J.L (33) N.F. ₤

The Essence of Bankim Chandra's
Krishna Charitra

The Essence of Bankim Chandra's
Krishna Charitra

Translated from Bengali by Alo Shome

HINDOOLOGY BOOKS

Published by

J-3/16, Daryaganj, New Delhi-110002
☎ 23276539, 23272783, 23272784 • *Fax:* 011-23260518
E-mail: info@pustakmahal.com • *Website:* www.pustakmahal.com

Sales Centre
10-B, Netaji Subhash Marg, Daryaganj, New Delhi-110002
☎ 23268292, 23268293, 23279900 • *Fax:* 011-23280567

Branch Offices
Bangalore: ☎ 22234025 • *Telefax:* 22240209
E-mail: pmblr@sancharnet.in • pustak@sancharnet.in
Mumbai: ☎ 22010941
E-mail: rapidex@bom5.vsnl.net.in
Patna: ☎ 3294193 • *Telefax:* 0612-2302719
E-mail: rapidexptn@rediffmail.com
Hyderabad: *Telefax:* 040-24737290
E-mail: pustakmahalhyd@yahoo.co.in

© Copyright : Hindoology Books
ISBN 978-81-223-1035-1
Edition : November 2008

The Copyright of this book, as well as all matter contained herein (including pictures) rests with the Publishers. No person shall copy the name of the book, its title design, matter, illustrations & photographs in any form and in any language, totally or partially or in any distorted form. Anybody doing so shall face legal action and will be responsible for damages.

Printed at : Param Offsetters, Okhla, New Delhi-110020

Dedicated to

The memory of my grandparents
Sri Nalin Bihari Dutt
&
Smt Salila Bala Dutt

Acknowledgements

Sincere thanks to Sri Ram Avtar Gupta, Chairman, Pustak Mahal, for supporting my project and encouraging me to complete it.

My homage to Mahamahopadhyaya Anantalal Thakur for translating Bankim Chandra's Sanskrit passages into English for my use.

Thanks to Manjushree Choudhary for her gracious assistance.

My gratitude to Sri Samir Kumar Shome, my husband, for his support, appreciation, encouragement and love.

Affection to my children and to other relatives and friends for their constant goodwill and understanding.

Special thanks to Sri Subas Maitra for his kind and optimistic appraisals, his steady guidance and insightful editorial skills.

Declaration

Bankim Chandra had written his book, Krishna Charitra, in the first person. All the interpretations in the book are Bankim Chandra's own. The translator does not take any credit for the opinions expressed in the narration, even when they are stated as 'I feel' or 'in my opinion'.

The translator's individual comments appear only in footnotes, Translator's Notes and Translator's Epilogue.

Contents

Life and Personality of Bankim Chandra   *13*
Introduction to Bankim Chandra's Krishna Charitra   *15*

Section I – The Beginning

The Purpose of My Work   *19*
How to Find the Real Krishna   *21*
The Mahabharata from Historical Point of View   *23*
The Pandavas   *25*
Interpolations and Distortions in the Mahabharata   *26*
The Unnatural and the Supernatural in the Mahabharata   *27*

Section II – Vrindavana

Yaduvansha (Sri Krishna's Ancestry)   *31*
Sri Krishna's Birth   *33*
Sri Krishna's Childhood   *35*
Sri Krishna's Adolescence   *37*
The Gopis of Vraja   *40*
Sri Radha   *42*
Closing of Vrindavana Lila   *47*

Section III – Mathura to Dwaraka

The Slaying of Kansa   *51*
Sri Krishna's Education   *54*
Jarasandha   *56*
Life in Dwaraka   *60*
Sri Krishna's Consorts   *61*

Section IV – Indraprastha

Draupadi's Swayamvara *67*

Report of Krishna's Meeting with Yudhisthira *70*

The Harana of Subhadra *72*

Fire in the Khandava Forest *77*

Krishna, the Humanitarian *80*

Krishna's Advice to Kill Jarasandha *82*

Account of Krishna's Meeting with Jarasandha *84*

The Duel of Bhima and Jarasandha *86*

The Ritual of Honouring the Best Person in the Assembly *89*

The Slaying of Shishupala *95*

Exile of the Pandavas *97*

Section V – Upaplavya

Warriors Choose their Sides *101*

Sanjaya's Mission *106*

Proposal of Krishna's Visit to Hastinapura *111*

The Journey *114*

Day One in Hastinapura *116*

Day Two in Hastinapura *119*

Krishna's Meeting with Karna *122*

Section VI – Kurukshetra

Bhishma in Battle *127*

Jayadratha Killed *130*

Understanding the Work of the Later Poets *133*

The Fall of Ghatotkacha *136*

The Fall of Drona *139*

The Religion that Krishna Preached *144*

The Fall of Karna *147*

The Fall of Duryodhana *150*

The Last Days of the War *154*

Setting up a Legislation *156*

Sermons on Desire *159*

Last Meeting with the Pandavas *161*

Section VII – The Incidents in Prabhasha

Annihilation of the Yadus *165*

Conclusion *170*

Translator's Epilogue *174*

Translator's Notes

A. *The Mahabharata and its Time* *175*

B. *The Caste System in India* *177*

C. *The Status of Women in Sri Krishna's Time* *179*

D. *How Bhakti was Perceived in Mahabharata's Time* *181*

E. *Some Critical Comments on Bankim Chandra's Krishna Charitra* *183*

Appendix

A. *Rabindranath Tagore's Criticism of Bankim Chandra's Krishna Charitra* *185*

B. *Bankim Chandra's Defence against Tagore's Criticism* *199*

C. *Bankim Chandra's Study of Sri Krishna in Literature* *203*

Life and Personality of Bankim Chandra

Bankim Chandra was the youngest of three sons of Durgasundari Devi and Jadav Chandra Chattopadhyaya. He was born in Kanthalapara, near Kolkata, on 26th June 1838. Jadav Chandra was a Deputy Magistrate and a man of culture. Sanjeev Chandra, one of Bankim's elder brothers, was a renowned writer, specially remembered for his fascinating travelogue, *Palamou*.

After a rigorous schooling in a convent school in Medinipur till July 1856, Bankim entered the Calcutta Presidency College to study law. In 1857, he took the very first entrance examination held by Calcutta University, clearing it in the first division. He appeared for the BA examination in 1858 but failed to clear one out of six papers – Bengali! Both he and Jadunath Basu were awarded the degree, however, as the first graduates of the University after being given seven grace marks each in Bengali. The examiner was Ishwar Chandra Vidyasagar.

After his studies, Bankim Chandra served the government as Deputy Magistrate and Deputy Collector and showed considerable proficiency in his work in spite of his periodic conflicts with the bureaucracy.

According to the custom in his time, he was married to a five-year-old girl when he himself was eleven. A decade later, one year after the death of his first wife, he married Rajlakshmi Devi, who became his true life partner.

Bankim's first novel, *Rajmohan's Wife* (1864), was in English. His first novel in Bengali, *Durgesh Nandani*, was published in 1865. Some of his other masterpieces are *Kapal Kundala, Mrinalini, Devi Chaudharani* and *Ananda Math*. Throughout his writing career, Bankim contributed excellent articles to various newspapers and magazines. His work covered many subjects – politics, economics, social sciences, religion, philosophy and popular science.

In 1891, Bankim took premature retirement from service on health reasons and devoted the rest of his life mainly to the study of religious subjects. He died on 8th April 1894 at the age of fifty-six.

Paying tribute to Bankim Chandra, Tagore said that he did not write for fame... but to express the noblest and the most beautiful thoughts of a cultured mind in the finest of words.

◆

Introduction to Bankim Chandra's Krishna Charitra

Sri Aurobindo had called Bankim Chandra a *rishi*.

In 1882, Reverend Hastie, a Scottish missionary, began to publish severe criticisms on Hinduism in *The Statesman*. Bankim decided to challenge his accusations. Under the pseudonym of Ram Chandra, he replied with vigour to the missionary's charges in the columns of the same paper. Until then, Bankim had made his name as a literary stylist. But from that time onwards, he turned more and more into a spiritual thinker. He devoted the last years of his life to examining the essence of religion and putting them in writing.

Sri Krishna is an enormous Indian icon for more than three thousand years. He represents love, devotion, wisdom and beauty. Bankim Chandra eagerly took up the study of Sri Krishna in India's vast cosmology. Bankim Chandra's *Krishna Charitra* is the longest and the most famous of his works in this category.

Krishna Charitra is a wonderful classic and a great work that showcases intense erudition. While translating, however, I have left out certain portions, some small and some large, of that wonderful effort, as I felt that, for the readers I have in mind, they would be too lengthy and obscure.

Bankim Chandra has been exceedingly thorough in his undertaking. He discusses roots of words at length to seek out their real meanings, compares statements by Sanskrit scholars, declares his own judgements on them, and reflects on philosophical concepts. He does all this to defend his thesis. Moreover, he simultaneously deals with the difficult task of convincing a large readership of 19th century Bengal, immersed in *Krishna-bhakti*, of the validity of his search for Sri Krishna, the real person, hidden behind centuries of myths and legends.

As it should be, Bankim explains his methodology in detail in Section I of his book. Here, he also discusses the sources of his research material. Section I is divided into seventeen chapters. I have specifically chosen to cut short this part (rephrased as Section I in this book) to reduce the overload of data which, I reiterate, a genuine thesis would need, but would be of little interest to the common readers. The other chapters of the book (from Section II to Section VII), however, have been translated in greater detail.

Then, in the course of his work, Bankim Chandra has often expressed his exasperation with the European people. These outbursts, however, are quite irrelevant after six decades of India's independence. So, most of such passages have also been omitted.

It is said that making a translation is like serving two masters at the same time. Languages do differ in their grammatical and syntactical structures. And, a translator must meet the demands of the receiving language, while remaining true to the source language. I dare to think that I have not made many compromises. The primary purpose of my effort is to present to the readers a specimen of Bankim's robust power of reasoning and to show what truth he found about his beloved deity. A comprehensive review of Bankim Chandra's *Krishna Charitra* by Rabindranath Tagore (in translation) and a few of my short notes have been attached to the present work to put the study in the right perspective.

A longer English translation of Bankim's *Krishna Charitra* (stretching up to 371 pages), done by Pradip Bhattacharya in 1991 and published by The M P Birla Foundation under the series 'Classics of the East', is recommended for readers who would love to have the thesis with all its details.

◆

Section - I
The Beginning

The Purpose of My Work

The majority of Hindus in India and almost all Hindus in Bengal believe that Sri Krishna is an *avatar* of God. In the province of Bengal, the worship of Krishna is widespread. Here, he is worshipped in the village temples and in the villagers' homes. Almost every month has a day reserved for his festival. There are ceremonies and Krishna-processions. There are singing of psalms and recitation of his name over and over again. People's clothing have the name of Krishna printed on them and people's bodies are anointed with his mark. Many Bengalis do not start even the writing of a note or a letter without super-scribing the page with his name. Beggars utter his name to receive alms. Even our pet birds are taught to sing, "*Radhe Krishna, Radhe Krishna!*" Krishna has a pervading presence in our province and indeed in our country.

If Bengalis really believe that Krishna is God incarnate, then there is no doubt that being immersed in Krishna-consciousness is the best way to promote *Dharma*. What can be more virtuous for a human being than remembering His glory with every breath? But, what is such believers' idea of God? How do they accept that their god was a butter-stealer as a baby and a womaniser in his youth and as an adult had deceived men like Dronacharya? Critics of Hinduism say that such unscientific approach to religion has only made the followers of Hinduism undependable and dishonest as a race. I have yet to come across a Bengali who has tried to refute these accusations.

As I myself am deeply devoted to Krishna, I took it upon myself to get acquainted with the true nature of my deity. I have studied the *Puranas* and the *Itihasas* in detail. As a result, I have found that a lot of what is commonly known about Krishna is false. What is hidden under the make-believe stories of my God is something absolutely pure, refined and magnificent. I have come to know that such an ideal character as Sri Krishna has no parallel in human history. To explain how I have come to this conclusion is one of the two objectives of my present work. The second objective is to show why he is rated as the greatest of the great Indian heroes.

◆

How to Find the Real Krishna

I assume that most of my readers are rational thinkers and do not believe that Krishna had descended on earth in a miraculous fashion.

The question is, what is the authenticity of Krishna's existence? Where are the proofs that a person called Krishna had ever lived on earth? If Krishna had really lived, is there a way of knowing what he was really like? Let us find the answers to these queries now.

Information about Sri Krishna can be found in the following ancient books:

1. *The Mahabharata* 2. *Harivansha* 3. *The Puranas*

Of these, the *Puranas* are comprised of 18 volumes. (People in our country generally believe that all the *Puranas* were written by the same author. However, their divergence in style, their repeating of the same stories in different ways in different volumes and other tell-tale-signs prove that they were indeed written or compiled by many scholars over long periods of time. It is possible that there was only one original *Purana* which later got variegated into parts.)

Among the volumes of the *Puranas*, some of them have no mention of Krishna at all. The following volumes have his references:

a. *The Brahma Purana*, b. *The Vishnu Purana*, c. *The Vayu Purana*, d. *The Srimad Bhagavata Purana*, e. *The Brahmavaivarta Purana*, f. *The Skanda Purana*, g. *The Vamana Purana*, h. *The Kurma Purana*

However, there is a noticeable difference between what is written about Krishna in the *Mahabharata* and in the other above mentioned books. What is related about him in the *Mahabharata* is not found in *Harivansha* or in any of the *Puranas*. One of the reasons for this is that the *Mahabharata* relates the story of the Pandavas and so the mention of Krishna there is incidental. His activities there are restricted to those of a friend of the Pandavas and as of one on whom the Pandavas always relied upon. And, of course, that is how it should be. A little more about Sri Krishna only comes there as references to other matters.

It is clearly mentioned in *Harivansha* that it was written specifically to project that part of Krishna's life, which had not been recorded in the *Mahabharata*. *Srimad Bhagavata Purana* also makes a similar claim. When Vyasa confided in Narada about his omission of not writing much about Krishna in the *Mahabharata*, Narada advised him to write a separate book dedicated to him.

We will accept that the *Mahabharata* originated before *Harivansha* or any of the *Puranas*. But does the *Mahabharata* contain any truth? If *Mahabharata* itself is totally fictitious, then we can hardly believe that later books like *Harivansha* and *Srimad Bhagavata*, which have a character from the *Mahabharata* as their hero, will contain any truth.

In my research to find out what truth, if any, is there in the *Mahabharata*, I had to face two types of challenges. On the one hand is the mindset of my countrymen, their tendency to accept all ancient Sanskrit scriptures as containing eternal truth composed by seers (*rishis*) who could not make a single mistake! On the other hand are the Western scholars who refuse to admit that the weak, servile people of the Hindu race could ever have had a glorious past. Most of them are engaged in undermining what is written in the Sanskrit scriptures. I have no need to criticise these 'great' men from the West for I write for my countrymen only. Unfortunately, a section of the literate Indians have become blind followers of the West. Without trying to find out the truth for themselves, they blindly trust the Western scholars for guidance. I dare to expect that a few from this group of Anglicised Indians will also read this book of mine and will judge Krishna's veracity for themselves.

❖

The Mahabharata from Historical Point of View

The *Mahabharata* is the first book in which Krishna appears. But can we accept the *Mahabharata* as a historical treatise when large parts of it narrate blurred, unnatural, impossible and ambiguous events? I argue that in spite of such absurd elements, we cannot dismiss the *Mahabharata* altogether as unhistorical. In our country, the *Mahabharata* has acquired the name of *Itihasa* from the time of its inception even though for the Europeans it is an epic and not history. There could be some valid reason for its being called *Itihasa*.[1] We can reject parts of the *Mahabharata* as fiction and yet accept the portions that are realistic.

In every civilisation, history and fiction have intermingled. If the *Mahabharata* contains more fantasy than history books of other countries, then there are also certain valid reasons for this.

Supernatural and unrealistic elements enter into historical treatises for two reasons. Firstly, the author himself includes substantial amount of hearsay in his work. Secondly, the text gets distorted and/or incorrectly interpreted with the passage of time.

Now, because of India's oral tradition, the history that is contained in the *Mahabharata* might have been more extensively mingled with unrealistic elements and hearsay. This is the first reason why the *Mahabharata* contains more fantasy than historical treatises of other ancient civilisations.

---

[1] *Translator's Footnote*
Itihasa – eeti ha asa – thus it happened

The second reason is that no historical document in the world has been as popular as the *Mahabharata* in the land of its origin. So the writers of the *Mahabharata* were more enthusiastically engaged in dramatising it for its audience.

Moreover, while the authors of other countries like Rome and Greece keenly protected the authenticity of what they had written by signing off their works, the ancient Indian authors generally did not put their names in their works and so did not mind it getting moulded into versions that would serve the common good better.

Ultimately, there are no valid reasons to believe that the *Mahabharata* does not contain any element of history.

◆

The Pandavas

After my studies of the ancient Sanskrit scriptures, I came to the conclusion that king Yudhisthira ruled 1115 years before Chandragupta (330 BC), the great emperor who confronted Alexander (356-323 BC) of Macedonia.

In the original version of the *Mahabharata*, there was no mention of the Pandavas. The German scholar Lasen believed that the war described in the *Mahabharata* was fought between the Kurus and the Panchalas. Lasen reasoned that the Pandavas were imaginary figures put in there. Even though I admit that the confrontation mentioned in the *Mahabharata* may have been mainly between the Kurus and the Panchalas, I do not accept that the Pandavas were non-existent, for it is quite possible and natural that the Pandavas – in their roles as the sons-in-law of the ruler of Panchala – would support him when he attacked Dhritarashtra and his people.

Another reason for which the European scholars have their doubts about the existence of the Pandavas is that no Sanskrit writing contemporary to the initial *Mahabharata* mentioned the Pandavas. To this, my answer is that this was simply because there was no tradition of history-writing in India. For example, no Indian book of Alexander's time recorded his Indian adventures. That does not prove that Alexander did not come to India.

On the whole, again, we do not have anything to conclusively prove that the Pandavas did not exist.

Interpolations and Distortions in the Mahabharata

The gist of what I said so far is that we have reasons to claim that the *Mahabharata* contains some history. And now, my job is to draw a character sketch of Sri Krishna based on that historical content of the *Mahabharata*. For this, I will select only those portions of the *Mahabharata*, which are convincingly historical and from those portions alone will select the biographical material about Krishna. What is absent in the *Mahabharata* but occurs in other books about Sri Krishna will also be considered, as some of these books – *Harivansha, Vishnu Purana* and *Srimad Bhagavata Purana* – were specially written to tell the story of that part of Sri Krishna's life, which was not covered in the *Mahabharata*. However, we shall keep in mind that the books which were written later than the *Mahabharata* at different periods of time by various authors will have lesser claim to history, and the later a book was written about Sri Krishna the more chances there will be of its having its facts distorted, for it is human nature to distort facts as time goes by.

◆

The Unnatural and the Supernatural in the Mahabharata

When we study the *Mahabharata* carefully, we find that it is constituted of three separate layers. The first layer is constructed by a skeletal story, which is more or less a historical document. The second layer is the elaborate version of the skeletal story where actual events are exaggerated for dramatic effects. The third layer consists of completely new stories added to the main theme.

Now, how to separate the core or the first layer of the *Mahabharata* from its other two layers? We shall do it by the following method:

- We shall reject any part of the *Mahabharata* that can be proved to be interpolated.
- We shall reject supernatural and unnatural events.
- Incidents that are not interpolated or do not seem to be unnatural but can be proved to be untrue in any other way shall also be rejected.

✦

Section - II
Vrindavana

Yaduvansha

(Sri Krishna's Ancestry)

In the 10th section of the *Rig Veda*, the name of Aau is mentioned. He was a king. Nahusa was Aau's son. Yayati was Aau's grandson born to Nahusa. Yayati begot five sons, the eldest being Yadu (generally believed to be the ancestor of Sri Krishna), the youngest Puru (generally believed to be the ancestor of Kauravas and Pandavas).

Even though we get the above information about the origin of a Yadu (believed to be Sri Krishna's ancestor) in the *Itihasas* and the *Puranas*, in *Harivansha*, there is a different story altogether. In that book, it is related that King Harasya of the Ikshwaku dynasty had once ruled Ayodhya. He had married Princess Madhumati of Madhuvana, better known as Mathura. For some reason, Harasya was expelled from Ayodhya and thus he came to live with his wife's family in Mathura. Their son, Yadu, later became a king.

Then, again somewhere else in the *Rig Veda*, the name Yadu appears as the name of a powerful non-Aryan ruler. Thus, we come upon three different persons having the name Yadu:

- Yadu, the son of Yayati
- Yadu of the Ikshwaku dynasty
- Yadu, the non-Aryan king

Which of these three was Krishna's ancestor?

We know it is generally accepted that Krishna's ancestor Yadu was the son of Yayati. Yet, as the Yadavas (Sri Krishna's clan) lived in Mathura and the Yadu of the Ikshwaku dynasty had connections with Mathura, we cannot conclusively rule out the possibility of Sri Krishna being the descendant of that Yadu.

In any case, we know for sure that kings Vrishni, Andhaka, Kukura and Bhoja along with some other rulers had the same ancestry as Krishna and their descendants had lived together in Mathura.

Sri Krishna's Birth

Vasudeva was Krishna's father, and Devaki his mother. Ugrasena's son Kansa was the ruler of the Yadavas at the time of Krishna's birth. Devaki was Kansa's sister or perhaps a cousin, for Devaki and Kansa had the same paternal grandfather. We all know that there is a popular myth surrounding Sri Krishna birth, according to which, while Vasudeva was bringing his bride Devaki home after their wedding, Kansa had lovingly offered to be their charioteer (*sarathi*). As the nuptial chariot was on the move, an oracle from the skies was suddenly heard announcing that the eighth child born from Devaki's womb would kill Kansa.

This forecast ruined Kansa's love for Devaki and he wanted to kill her then and there. Vasudeva calmed him down by promising that he himself would hand over to Kansa every child that would be born of his marriage with Devaki. At this, Kansa spared Devaki's life but kept both husband and wife in jail. He killed their first six children one after the other, just after birth. The seventh child that Devaki had conceived got miraculously transferred to Vasudeva's other wife Rohini's womb whom Vasudeva had left with his relative Nanda, a milkman and lived not very far from Mathura with a band of cowherds.

This child was born as Balarama. Devaki's eighth child, Krishna, was born one stormy night. Vasudeva secretly carried him to Rohini and in exchange brought back the daughter whom Nanda's wife Yashoda had given birth to that same night. He offered this child to Kansa as his own and Devaki's. When Kansa tried to destroy this girl child, she disappeared in the skies prophesying that the baby that would slay Kansa was already born and was growing elsewhere safely.

The historical facts that we may extract from the given accounts are as follows:

Krishna was born of Devaki in the clan of the Yadavas in Mathura. His father was Vasudeva. Since infancy, Krishna was left in the care of Nanda. The reason behind Vasudeva's putting baby Krishna in Nanda's care to be raised in secret was, most probably, Kansa's cruelty towards the Yadavas. For Kansa, like Aurangzeb, had dethroned his own father to become the ruler of his clan. His ruthless behaviour had forced many Yadavas to migrate from Mathura where he held his sway. In the *Mahabharata* and in the *Bhagavata Purana*, Krishna himself spoke of Kansa's brutal nature. It is, therefore, reasonable that Vasudeva should keep his first wife Rohini and her child Balarama away from Mathura under the protection of a trusted relative. Similarly, it is logical to believe that Krishna, too, should be sent to Nanda's household for the sake of safety.

✦

Sri Krishna's Childhood

The *Puranas* relate a number of legends that surround Krishna's childhood. Let us discuss them one by one:

1. The Killing of Putana

The story goes that a *Rakshasi* called Putana was sent by Kansa to Nanda's home to kill Sri Krishna. She entered the house disguised as a lissom beauty. However, her breasts had been smeared with poison. But the infant Krishna tortured her so much while sucking her milk that Putana lost her life. At the time of death, she regained her own self, her corpse spreading over six *Kroshas* of land.

The above story could have originated from the following fact:

'Putana' was the name of an illness that new-born babies were said to contact in Krishna's time. The baby who could suck hard at the breast of his mother or nurse and feed himself well even when affected by Putana would be a survivor. Possibly, killing of Putana is an allegory of Krishna's surviving this childhood affliction.

2. Overturning the Cart

Krishna's foster mother Yashoda (Nanda's wife) had put Krishna under a cart. But, even as an infant that he was, he pushed the cart down with his tiny feet.

The story could have originated from a similar tale in the *Rig Veda* as there is reason to believe that the *Vedas* had influenced the legends of Krishna's life. It is possible that it was borrowed from the legend of Indra's breaking of Usha's cart that is told in the *Rig Veda*.

3. Baby Krishna Eating Mud and Showing the Universe to his Mother

Baby Krishna had put some mud in his mouth. When Yashoda made him open his mouth, he transformed into a miraculous being showing mother Yashoda the Universe in his own open mouth.

We find this story for the first time in the *Bhagavata*. It does not appear in any earlier reference of Sri Krishna's life. So, quite possibly it was conceived by the author of the *Bhagavata*.

4. Trinavarta

An *Asura* named Trinavarta had once taken baby Krishna into the skies.

From the detailed description of the incident, it appears that Trinavarta was quite simply a gust of whirlwind. In fact, the *Bhagavata* mentions that the *Asura* had taken the shape of a gust of wind. And, it may not be totally impossible for a gust of powerful wind to lift up an infant for a while. This anecdote, too, appears first in the *Bhagavata* and has only a slim chance of carrying any truth.

5. The Stories of Krishna Stealing Butter and Teasing the Gopis

There is reference to these stories in *Harivansha*. In the *Bhagavata*, however, they take an exaggerated form.

The basic message hidden behind these stories is that Krishna was a concerned and generous person who loved animals (because he fed the monkeys what he took from the *gopis*) and humans alike.

6. Krishna's Uprooting of Twin Kurchi Trees

This anecdote appears even in the *Mahabharata*, Shishupala referring to it. Kurchi trees do not grow much and can be as small as shrubs. In the *Bhagavata*, however, the trees are made to become the sons of Kubera who had turned into trees as the result of a curse and are freed by Sri Krishna's touch!

When Krishna was still a tiny child growing up in the household of Nanda and Yashoda, Nanda and many of his friends left the homestead they were sharing and resettled in Vrindavana. Probably Vrindavana was chosen simply because it was a better place to live in or because – as is related in *Harivansha* – their old habitation had got infested by wolves.

Sri Krishna's Adolescence

The description of Vrindavana has a unique place in creative literature. However, our task is to cull from that description pieces of reality to document Sri Krishna's life.

The author of the *Bhagavata* says that Krishna killed three *Asuras* after coming to Vrindavana. They were Vatsasura, Bakasura and Aghasura, i.e. one looking like a calf, another looking like a bird (vulture), and the third looking like a snake. It would not have been impossible for a brave and sturdy young lad to kill such creatures to protect his friends. However, there is no mention of these events in the *Vishnu Purana*, the *Mahabharata* or the *Harivansha*. However, we can recognise a faint similarity to them in a prayer to fire in *Yajur Veda*:

"Oh, *Agni*, destroy them who are cheaters, who are jealous, who are too ready to find faults with us, who are killers."

When the author of the *Bhagavata* conceived the allegorical story of Krishna subduing three *Asuras*, was he influenced by the prayer to *Agni* in the *Yajur Veda*?

Then, in the *Bhagavata*, Lord Brahma tested Krishna by making all the cows and the cowherds vanish. Krishna instantly created a fresh set of cows and cowherds. This must be, just to say, in a manner of speaking, that even Brahma was unable to correctly judge Krishna's abilities.

Then, one day Krishna drank forest fire to save his people. For the *Shaivas*, there is the story of Shiva drinking poison to save the earth. Was Krishna made to outdo Shiva by drinking fire? (It should be remembered that there was rivalry between *Shaiva* and *Vaishnava* sects. So, one can guess how exaggerating the feats of each other's gods could easily become a common practice.)

Now, let us take up the *Kaliadamana* story:

A poisonous snake named Kalia lived with his large family in a pool formed by river Yamuna. In the *Vishnu Purana*, the snake had three hoods, in *Harivansha* it had five hoods, in the *Bhagavata Purana* it had a thousand. Because of their venom, nobody could live in the vicinity of that part of Yamuna and many a cattle and cowherd had dropped dead after drinking water drawn from that pool. No plant could grow on the banks and even birds that flew over that poisonous tract got struck. So, Krishna wished to overpower Kalia and rid Vrindavana of its torments. He leaped into the river to fight Kalia who immediately attacked him. So Krishna jumped on Kalia's hoods. Holding his flute to his lips, he began to dance his cowherd-dance. Thus tortured, Kalia began to bleed through his mouths. His many wives, now, prayed for mercy. Responding to their prayer, Sri Krishna released Kalia but ordered him to leave Vrindavana forever with his family to start living in the sea. Thus Yamuna's water was purified.

In essence, the above story is a beautiful allegory of a brave, strong and righteous young boy destroying the evils that afflict human existence. And, on its own, that impressive description of Sri Krishna set on the hoods of Kalia is a remarkable artistic creation by its composers. Looking at a sculpted statue of that wonderful image, who would have the heart to snub a Hindu for being an idol-worshipper?

The fact that is hidden behind the myth of Krishna holding up *Giri Govardhana* for seven days to protect Vrindavana from a deluge is more interesting and relevant to our day-to-day living.

The story goes that the people of Vrindavana used to hold an elaborate worship of Indra, the rain-god, every year. Once, Sri Krishna pointed out the futility of such a ritual. "Take care of what is around us, instead", he said, "Let us just look after our cattle well and let us conserve the flora and fauna of *Govardhana*. Let us care for our own habitat."

The people of Vrindavana listened to their young leader and abstained from holding Indra worship that year. The disappointed Indra, in his anger, brought so much rain there that it threatened to destroy the whole settlement. So, Krishna dislodged *Govardhana* from its base and held it over Vrindavana like a huge umbrella. After seven days, Indra admitted defeat and resumed cordial relationship with Krishna.

Giri Govardhana still exists. It is a small hill. This hill has a strange look, as if it had been uprooted by some natural force and was again reinstated. Maybe the hill had turned this way thousands of years ago in the course of time, giving rise to the myth of Krishna having uprooted and replaced it.

There is reference to this myth even in the *Mahabharata* when Shishupala tauntingly said that Krishna had lifted the anthill like *Govardhana* (the hill, though, was not an anthill but a real hillock). But as we had agreed earlier, supernatural elements contained even in the *Mahabharata* must be taken as entering the work from time to time and co-existing there along with the facts. The important point the story makes is that Sri Krishna had tried to convince his people of the need of looking after their natural habitat.

✦

The Gopis of Vraja

A worshipper of Krishna focuses on his deity's relationship with the *gopis* (milkmaids) as one of the vital components of his religion. For the rivals of the Krishna cult, however, this relationship is repulsive. For them it is the worst blemish in Krishna's character.

In the *Mahabharata*, there is no mention of the *gopis*. In this book, in the chapter called *Sabha Parva*, Shishupala, the Krishna-hater, recites a lengthy monologue describing the faults of Krishna. If Sri Krishna's excesses with the *gopis* were known at the time of the *Mahabharata* or at the time this tract of the *Mahabharata* was written, Shishupala would have certainly commented on it. So, we can conclude that the tales of Sri Krishna's promiscuity and lovemaking with the *gopis* were created afterwards.

Nevertheless, the word *gopijanapriya* (the beloved of the *gopis*) was used by Draupadi in her prayer to Krishna when she was being disrobed. This is quite natural. In Vrindavana, ever since his childhood, Krishna was loved by one and all – men and women alike. He had a pleasing personality. He must have been a handsome youth in his growing years. And, young people, girls and boys, collecting together and dancing or just spending time together, each having girlfriends and boyfriends of their own is a natural aspect of human behaviour that is usually accepted without fuss both in civilised and uncivilised societies.

It is acceptable, therefore, that Krishna was a beloved boyfriend of the *gopis*. From time to time, however, in many societies, mixing with the opposite sex is objected to and sometimes even the slightest intimacy is criticised. It seems to me that in Krishna's lifetime, Vrindavana was a free society in this respect and his friendship with the *gopis* was not a matter of criticism.

Later, the society changed. When the stories of Krishna's life were retold, his friendship with the *gopis* took on a different colour. Mysticism was added to the facts by Krishna-worshippers and philosophies were built on it to explain away this facet of Sri Krishna's life. Additionally, under the cover of mysticism and philosophy, *Raas Leela* (dancing of boys and girls holding hands) of Krishna and the *gopis* was set free to take many imaginative formats.

♦

Sri Radha

Of all the ancient books that refer to Sri Krishna, the name of Sri Radha occurs only in two — *Brahmavaivarta Purana* and in the works of poet Jaidev. Some scholars have brought in Radha again and again in their discourses on *Bhagavata*, even though there is no mention of Radha in the original book.

The *Bhagavata* describes how some *gopis* react on spotting footprints disappearing into a bush. Overwhelmed with jealousy, they assume that Krishna has gone into the bush with his favourite girlfriend. However, this is only an assumption of the *gopis* through which the author of this tract of the *Bhagavata* highlights how dearly loved Krishna was among the *gopis*. No name is mentioned. So, there is no basis to think that Krishna's partner was Radha at that time.

There is no mention of Radha in the original *Bhagavata* or in *Vishnu Purana*, *Harivansha* or the *Mahabharata*. Yet, today Radha is the most important element in Krishna-worship. Now, Krishna's name is always paired with Radha. There is no Krishna-temple without Radha in it. And in Vaishnava literature, Radha even has a greater significance than Sri Krishna himself.

Now, if Radha is not available in the *Mahabharata*, *Harivansha*, *Vishnu Purana* or the *Bhagavata*, then where did she originate from? Let us try to find out.

We meet Radha for the first time in *Brahmavaivarta Purana*, which, according to the Englishman Wilson, is the latest of the *Puranas*. To complicate matters further, the original *Brahmavaivarta Purana* is now lost. What is available today records a peculiar hierarchy of gods which is quite different from the generally accepted one.

It is commonly understood that Krishna is an *avatar* of Vishnu. But in the *Brahmavaivarta Purana* that is available to us, it is the other way round! Here, Krishna is the creator of Vishnu and all other gods and living creatures. Here, *Golokdhama*, the place where Sri Krishna lived, has a higher status than Vishnu's *Vaikuntha*! We find Radha for the first time in this heavenly *Golokdhama*, established as its dominant goddess. (The description of *Golokdhama*, however, is a shameless imitation of the descriptions of Vrindavana poetically composed by the authors of earlier books.)

In this new *Brahmavaivarta Purana*, there is another important character called Viraja who is a rival of Radha for Sri Krishna's love. In this version, Krishna goes to Viraja's house, which makes Radha angry and jealous. She follows him in her chariot and comes to Viraja's house, too. Viraja's watchman, Sridama, however does not allow her to enter. Inside, though, Viraja gets so scared of Radha that she melts and becomes a river.

Krishna promptly revives her and gives her back her original form. Their intense lovemaking, by and by, results in the birth of seven sons, whom their mother's curse turns into seven seas. The mother curses them because they disturb her in her lovemaking. Radha, on hearing of this romance admonishes Krishna and punishes him with a curse that would force him to be born on earth. At this, Sridama, the watchman, who is a devotee of Sri Krishna, rebukes Radha which infuriates her. Radha curses him too to be born as an *Asura*. Sridama takes his revenge by cursing Radha to be born as a human female who would acquire infamy for her loose character. Later, both Sridama and Radha pray to Krishna to save them from each other's curses. Krishna blesses Sridama with the boon that he would be the king of the *Asuras*. And he consoles Radha by promising that when she goes to earth, he himself would follow her.

Even though the weird stories mentioned above were written in comparatively recent times, they dominate the minds of the Bengali people. They have become the source-material for Bengali Vaishnava poets like Jaidev. They have also given rise to passionate songs and *yatra*-plays.

Yet, strangely, an important point mentioned in *Brahmavaivarta Purana* has been ignored by the Bengalis. The *Purana* holds that Sri Krishna and Radha were married couples. But today, they are generally understood as unwed lovers.

Let me relate how Radha and Krishna were married as described in *Brahmavaivarta Purana*. For this, we have to remember that (according to *Brahmavaivarta Purana*), Radha was older to Krishna by several years as she was forced to be born on earth some years before Sri Krishna followed her. Radha was a young girl when Krishna was a baby.

Once Nanda was grazing his cows in a Vrindavana field. Baby Krishna was with him. Nanda offered his cows the clear and sweet-tasting water of the pond and he drank some of it himself. Then, holding Krishna to his breast, he sat down under a banyan tree. Krishna, tiny though he was, miraculously covered the sky with dark clouds. The fields became shadowy. A strong wind rose. The clap of thunder was heard. It began to rain heavily and the trees fell uprooted.

Nanda was scared, "How can I go home without my cattle? And if I don't go home now, what will happen to this infant?" As Nanda was speaking thus to himself, Krishna began to weep holding on to Nanda's neck as if he were afraid of the surroundings. At this moment, Radha appeared. Nanda was amazed by her grace and beauty. He welcomed her, saying, "I have heard from Garga that you are Hari's favourite. And this is Mahavishnu. I am myself an ordinary human being charmed by his *Maya*. My Lady, here, please accept your beloved. Go with him wherever you would be happy. Later, when your wishes are satisfied, give him back to me, again, as my son."

Nanda thus offered Krishna to Radha and she carried him away. Selecting a place of her liking, she recalled a dancing ground. Immediately a beautiful garden transpired. When Radha put Krishna down, he instantly took the form of a handsome youth. Addressing Radha he said, "If you remember *Goloka*, I am here to keep my promise."

Brahma appeared on the scene at that moment. After paying his respects to Radha, he took upon himself the responsibility of giving her away to Sri Krishna in marriage according to Vedic rituals. After completing the wedding ceremonies, Brahma disappeared.

The above account of Radha and Krishna's wedding is related in *Brahmavaivarta Purana* and readers will find that the author of that treatise distorts the very facts on which *Vaishnava Dharma* (with Vishnu as its central figure) was originally based. Radha becomes the centre of the transformed *Vaishnava Dharma* and gives a new interpretation to the story of Sri Krishna's life. Jaidev based his *Gitagovinda* on this new interpretation.

Other *Vaishnava* poets of Bengal – including Vidyapati and Chandidasa – followed Jaidev's example when they wrote their devotional songs of Krishna. Even Sri Chaitanya Deva structured his fascinating philosophy of *Bhaktivada* on this innovative *Vaishnava Dharma*. So, it would not be an exaggeration to say that *Brahmavaivarta Purana* has influenced Bengali thought-process and Bengali lifestyle as no other poet, *Rishi, Shastra* or *Purana* has.

Let us now examine the underlying message of this new stream of *Vaishnava Dharma* and try to find out the reason for its being launched:

Among the various philosophical thoughts developed in India, six are better known than the others. Of these six, again, Vedanta Philosophy and Sankhya Philosophy are the more popular ones. The origin of Vedanta Philosophy is found in the *Upanishads* and is based on the theory of monotheism. It holds that God is omnipresent and manifests Himself in each and every thing in the Universe. God is the Supreme Being and other beings are His manifestations. That a being is different from Him is an illusion and liberation from this illusion is our salvation.

The above theory contained in the *Vedanta* constituted the basis of the earlier *Vaishnava* religion. Vishnu and his *avatar* Krishna are both Vedantic gods. In the *Shanti Parva* of the *Mahabharata*, Bhishma's prayer to Krishna exemplifies this monotheistic theory of the Vedanta.

However, even monotheism can be explained in various ways. In later years, Shankaracharya, Ramanujacharya, Madhavacharya and Ballabhacharya, by their individual explanations have created four different views of monotheism, namely, *Advaitavada, Visistadvaitavada, Dvaitadvaitavada* and *Vishuddhadvaitavada*. In ancient times, however, when the *Vedanta* was still new, so many approaches to monotheism had not existed. In those days, relationship of God and the Universe was described in either of the following ways:

A. There is nothing that is not God. God is contained in everything.

B. God is not the Universe or vice-versa, but the Universe is contained in God. God Himself is inexhaustible. He stretches beyond the Universe.

Earlier *Vaishnava* religion was based on the second (B) approach to Vedantic monotheism. *Vaishnava* religion that emerged later, as expounded in *Brahmavaivarta Purana*, does not follow the Vedantic principle of monotheism at all. It is structured on a totally different philosophy – the Sankhya philosophy.

Sankhya Philosophy is based on the theory that Nature and Supreme Consciousness are two different entities. Sankhya philosophers named them *Prakriti* and *Purusha*.

The theory of *Prakriti* and *Purusha* also became the basis of *Tantrika* faith where coming together of those two forces was believed to be desirable. In Tantricism, *Prakriti* (Nature or instinct) was given a lot of importance and was likened to feminine desire while *Purusha* (consciousness or intelligence) was supposed to be masculine wisdom. Because it advocated free mixing of men and women, Tantricism easily appealed to the masses.

Dissatisfied with the *Vaishnava* theory of *Advaitavada*, many devotees turned to *Tantrika* faith where men and women could mix freely. The *Vaishnavas* had to do something to compete with the *Tantrikas'* popularity. What they did was clever. They picked up the substance of *Tantrika* theory and infused it into their own religion. The author of *Brahmavaivarta Purana* revived or rejuvenated *Vaishnava Dharma* by creating Radha and making her as important as *Prakriti* of the *Tantrikas*.

❖

Closing of Vrindavana Lila

In *Bhagavata Purana*, there are a few more episodes about Krishna's childhood:

While Nanda was bathing in the Yamuna one day, Lord Varuna's people caught him and took him away to their master's palace. Krishna followed them there and rescued Nanda. This story seems to suggest that Krishna had once saved Nanda from drowning in the Yamuna.

A snake once held Nanda in his mouth. When Krishna killed the snake and rescued Nanda, it miraculously turned into a scholar and went home. This happened, it is related, because the scholar was trapped into the snake awaiting his release through Krishna's touch. This story may simply mean that Krishna had once saved Nanda from the attack of a serpent.

When an *Asura* called Shankhachuda had abducted the women of *Vraja*, Krishna and Balarama had chased him off and rescued the ladies.

The above incidents are not mentioned in *Vishnu Purana*, *Harivansha* or the *Mahabharata*, but there is mention of Krishna's slaying of the demons Keshi and Arishta in each the three books. In the *Mahabharata*, the reference comes up during Shishupala's intense berating of Krishna in the beginning of Yudhisthira's *Ashwamedha Yajna*. The demons, Arishta and Keshi, were bull-shaped and horse-shaped respectively, and interestingly, in the *Mahabharata*, Shishupala simply refers to them as a bull and a horse.

To conclude Section II of my book, which consists of Sri Krishna's life in Vrindavana, I ask this question to my readers and to myself: What data can we collect about Krishna's life from this tract? The historical facts that we collect from it is only the following:

Scared of the tyrant Kansa, Vasudeva put his wife Rohini and his sons Balarama and Krishna secretly under the care of his relative Nanda in his house. Krishna's childhood and adolescence were spent there. Krishna was a beautiful and pleasing child whom everybody loved. Even in his adolescence, he was strong-bodied and brave-hearted. He protected the cowherds of Vrindavana from harmful animals. From his earliest years, he was kind to all beings. He tried to help people in need. He was popular among the cowherds and the milkmaids. He enjoyed their company and had fun with them. His sense of *Dharma* was keen.

I cannot say with certainty, however, that what little I have mentioned above is all true or factual. I can only admit that nothing else can even be considered as true.

The notion that Krishna was a womaniser in his adolescence and youth does not seem to have a strong foundation.

◆

Section - III
Mathura to Dwaraka

The Slaying of Kansa

Kansa received the news that Krishna and Balarama had grown up into two brave and sturdy boys in Vrindavana and they had killed Putana and Arishta – two of his loyal followers. Devarshi Narada revealed to him that Krishna and Balarama were actually Vasudeva's own sons. Also that the child he had killed believing to be Devaki's eighth child was in fact a daughter born to Nanda and Yashoda. Vasudeva had exchanged Krishna for that infant so that Krishna could grow up safely with Nanda's family.

These scary revelations made Kansa furious. He cursed Vasudeva and resolved to kill him. He sent Akrura, one of the leaders of the Yadavas, to bring Krishna and Balarama to him from Vrindavana. He also started a *Yajna* called *Dhanurmukha* with his famous wrestlers to strengthen them for the killing of Krishna and Balarama.

In course of time, Akrura entered the kingdom with Krishna and Balarama captured. On their way to Mathura, they had a strange experience. An ugly woman with a hump had turned into a beautiful lady after Sri Krishna had touched her.

The strange incident is presented in a more ornate style in *Bhagavata Purana* and *Brahmavaivarta Purana*. In *Vishnu Purana*, though, it appears in a matter-of-fact way. Not only in this case but on all occasions, we find that among all the books we are dealing with, *Bhagavata Purana* contains the most unbelievable and unnatural stories. So, from now on we would not make any reference to *Bhagavata Purana*. The reason we referred to it till this point of our work is that its description of Krishna's childhood in Vrindavana is immensely popular. So, we could not ignore it altogether.

On their arrival in Kansa's kingdom, Krishna and Balarama were taken to the stadium where they killed Kansa's trained elephant Kuvalayapida and the famous wrestlers Chanura and Mustika. Seeing this havoc, Kansa ordered Nanda to be imprisoned in an iron enclosure and Vasudeva to be killed. Then, he ordered Krishna and Balarama to be chased away. On hearing this, Krishna jumped on the dais of the stadium from where Kansa and his courtiers were watching the events. He pulled Kansa down by his hair on to the stadium floor and killed him. Later, paying his respects to the elders present there, he crowned Ugrasena, Kansa's father, as the king of the land.

Harivansha and the various *Puranas* have the given story to tell about Kansa's death. However, even though we accept the slaying of Kansa as a historical fact, we reject the related details of the event that are given here because they consist mostly of supernatural elements. We know that Narada (who brought the news to Kansa that Krishna was alive) is a fictitious character and the oracle (which was the cause of Kansa's fear of Krishna to begin with) could not have transpired in reality. Besides, it is hard to believe that two young cowherds, Krishna and Balarama, had defeated the ruler of Mathura so easily.

Let us now examine what is written about the incident in the *Mahabharata*, the earliest book to contain this story. In the *Sabha Parva* of the *Mahabharata*, Krishna relates his own past to Yudhisthira, "...After a while Kansa, on defeating the Yadavas married Sahadeva and Anuja, the daughters of Brahadratha (Jayadratha). The tyrant made himself the leader of our clan. Some elderly *Kshatriyas* of Bhoja lineage, then, taking note of the cruelties of Kansa, advised me to migrate elsewhere, leaving my people behind. But, instead, after giving Akrura the daughter of Ahuka in marriage, Balabhadra and I killed Kansa and Sunama to give respite to our community."

In the above passage, it is not mentioned that Krishna-Balarama had arrived from Vrindavana to killed Kansa. In fact, there is even a faint suggestion that the brothers were already staying in Mathura, for we find Krishna mentioning that the elders of the clan had advised him to leave Mathura to save his own life.

It is not mentioned in Krishna's account of the event whether anyone besides his elder brother Balarama had helped him in the task of killing Kansa. But it can be understood from what Krishna said that at least the other Yadavas had not sided with Kansa. It seems to us that because everyone was tired of Kansa's cruelty, they had joined force under the leadership of Balarama and Krishna, the brothers who had impressed one and all with their physical prowess and other qualities, to kill Kansa. Logically, we cannot deduct anything more from Krishna's words in this context.

What historical data we safely collect from this part of our research is simply that after the Yadavas killed Kansa under the leadership of Krishna (amply helped by Balarama), Kansa's father Ugrasena was re-established on the throne.

The point to note here is that Sri Krishna and the other Yadavas made Ugrasena the ruler because the crown rightfully belonged to him. Though Krishna was superior to the other Yadavas in many respects, he never aspired for the throne because he was a *dharmatma* – a dutiful being. He never took advantage of situations but only did whatever duty demanded. We will also find in the following chapters how Krishna's *Dharma* consisted of doing only that which would help the community.

The episode of the slaying of Kansa by the Yadavas reveals to us several important characteristics of Krishna's character. We find that he possessed physical strength, that he was competent in whatever he undertook to do, that he was just and ever conscious of *Dharma*, that he took active interest in the well-being of others, and that he tried to improve the lot of his community.

Sri Krishna's Education

From the *Puranas*, we find that after Kansa's death, Krishna and Balarama came to Varanasi to take lessons under Sandipana *rishi*. Finishing their course of study in 64 days and paying their fees (*gurudakshina*), they returned to Mathura. This lesson was about the use of some arms.

Except this stint with Sandipana *rishi*, nothing else is documented about Krishna's education in any of the *Puranas* or *Itihasas*. There is no mention of Krishna taking any lessons when he was staying with Nanda's family. And yet Nanda belonged to the *Vaishya* caste, having the right to learn the Vedas. So it would be strange if Sri Krishna was not taught when he was with Nanda. Does this mean that Krishna had left Nanda's family before he was old enough to begin his studies?

Earlier we have mentioned how in *Sabha Parva* of the *Mahabharata*, Krishna relates his own past to Yudhisthira. This passage seems to indicate that Krishna did not come to Mathura to kill Kansa but was already staying there when the incident took place. Then, in the famous passage in the *Mahabharata* where Shishupala was bent upon demeaning Krishna, the former called him as one who consumed Kansa's grains (*Annabhoji*). This, too, suggests that perhaps Krishna left Vrindavana even as he was a child and was a resident of Mathura in his youth. From this, we may also come to the conclusion that much of what is said of young Krishna's intimacy with the milkmaids of Vrindavana is fictitious.

What kind of education Krishna had in Mathura is also not clear except the 64 days with Sandipana *rishi*. Readers who are convinced that Krishna was an incarnation of God may argue that being divine and thus all powerful, he did not require any education. But then, we might ask such readers, why did he require to spend even 64 days in training with Sandipana *rishi*?

Divine or not, we find, again and again, that Sri Krishna observed *Dharma* of a human being and executed his duties with humanly qualities. We have said this repeatedly and shall continue to reiterate this with more examples to support our belief. Now, to acquire efficiency in human terms, one has to develop one's abilities through education and training. That Krishna also had to be trained is proved by his apprenticeship under Sandipana *rishi*. And, we have evidence to believe that Sri Krishna had studied elsewhere too. We know that he had mastered the Vedas. One of Bhishma's reasons for selecting Krishna for the highest honour at Yudhisthira's *Rajasuya Yajna* was that he was a distinguished Vedic scholar. In the *Mahabharata*, there are several instances of Krishna's Vedic erudition. This erudition had not come to him by itself. In *Chhandogya Upanishad*, I have found evidence of Krishna having studied under the tutelage of *Rishi* Ghora of Angirasa lineage.

In Sri Krishna's time, the finishing phase of a scholar's higher education was called *Tapasya*. We get to hear of many great saintly monarchs observing *Tapasya* at certain periods of their lives. I found that what we understand as *Tapasya* now is not exactly what it was meant to connote in the Vedic times. To us, *Tapasya* means keeping a fast, sitting in the forest with closed eyes, controlling one's breathing and meditating about God. But, we hear that many among the gods themselves including Shiva had performed *Tapasya*. We cannot be sure as to what exactly the word meant in ancient times. Maybe it applied to a certain process of self-controlled endeavour towards developing one's innate abilities.

It is stated in the *Mahabharata* that Krishna had performed *Tapasya* for ten long years in the Himalayas. It is also written in the *Aisika Parva* of the *Mahabharata* that when as a result of Asvatthama's application of the *Brahmashira* weapon, Uttara was about to miscarry, Krishna was determined to revive the still-born foetus if need be. He had proudly told Asvatthama, "You just watch the power of my *Tapasya*."

Thus, we find indications that Sri Krishna was highly educated. His conduct and bearing also carried the mark of being a learned person. Unfortunately, we have been unable to fathom the exact nature of that erudition.

Jarasandha

*W*hen we study the history of India, we find that in earlier times in this country, or at least in its Northern part, an emperor would usually have his stronghold over other lesser rulers. Some of these lesser rulers would be paying taxes to the emperor while others would simply be acting upon his orders without paying taxes. In wartime, all of these petty rulers would help their lord.

In Sri Krishna's time, Jarasandha of Magadha had the emperor status in Northern India. Stories about his prowess and might are told in the *Mahabharata*, *Harivansha* and the *Puranas*. We can make a guess of his power by the fact that while both sides of the Kurukshetra war together consisted of eighteen *aksauhinis* of warriors, Jarasandha alone had twenty *aksauhinis* of warriors.

Kansa was Jarasandha's son-in-law. He had married two of the latter's daughters. And as Kansa's father-in-law, Jarasandha was the Yadavas' enemy. The Yadavas had to migrate from Mathura to Dwaraka because of the threat Jarasandha had posed for them.

However, we find some differences in what the *Mahabharata* tells us about Jarasandha's confrontation with the Yadavas and what is given about the matter in *Harivansha* and the *Puranas*. Let us first check out the latter books.

According to them, after Kansa's death, the two widowed sisters, wanting revenge for their husband's murder came crying to their father. Moved by their sorrow, Jarasandha invaded Mathura with a large army. More than anything else, he wanted to finish Krishna. The Yadavas had a light army but under the leadership of Krishna were able to resist the attack and even force their invaders to return. However, Jarasandha's army was so large and powerful that it was impossible for the Yadavas to really weaken him when he continued to attack Mathura at regular intervals. Even though he was pushed back every time, the assaults began to take a huge toll of the Yadavas' lives and other resources. Their army was diminishing fast and seemed as if it would be vanquished altogether.

After Jarasandha's seventeenth attack, the Yadavas, on Krishna's advice, decided to leave Mathura. They determined to migrate to a strategically safer place where they could build fortresses to protect themselves and chose an island called Dwaraka. Here, they started constructing residential houses and a range of garrisons, but Jarasandha's eighteenth attack came about before their rehabilitation was complete.

In the *Mahabharata*, Krishna himself speaks about the Yadavas' frustrations over their neighbour Jarasandha's rise in power but does not say that they were invaded eighteen times. In the *Sabha Parva* of the *Mahabharata*, where Krishna describes his past life, he says to Yudhisthira:

"...After a while, Kansa on defeating the other Yadavas, took away Sahadeva and Anuja, the daughters of Brahadratha (Jayadratha). That rascal, by suppressing his own people with sheer physical strength, became the mightiest amongst us. The elder *Kshatriyas* of the *Bhoja* lineage, therefore, advised me to leave the clan to save my own life.... I, thereafter, with Balabhadra's help, killed Kansa and Sunama. Our respite was short-lived, however, for very soon we found that Jarasandha had become oppressively powerful. And so, after discussing the issue with our friends and relatives, we came to the conclusion that it would be impossible to subdue him even if we fought him for three hundred years! Two divinely brave warriors, Hansa and Dimbaka, were Jarasandha's staunch supporters. No weapon was good enough to destroy them. I was certain that if these two and Jarasandha came together, they could conquer the three worlds! Oh Dharmaraja, it wasn't that this opinion was ours alone. Other neighbouring rulers also felt the same.

At that time, there was a king who was also named Hansa. Baladeva had killed him in a battle. When Dimbaka heard this, he mistook the slain Hansa to be his own closest friend. Grief-stricken, he killed himself by drowning in the Yamuna. Likewise, when Dimbaka heard what his friend had done, grieving for him, he too lost all desire for living and ended his life in the Yamuna. These two deaths hurt Jarasandha so badly that he lost all interest in conquests and returned home. The threat from Jarasandha thus removed, we happily resumed our normal life in Mathura. Unfortunately, soon after, the two widowed daughters of Jarasandha (who were married to Kansa) came to their father and urged him to kill their husband's murderer. This news disturbed us greatly, for we already had an estimate of Jarasandha's strength. So we decided on a strategic retreat from Mathura after dividing our common assets among ourselves.

We migrated westward and at present are living in the west in a settlement called Kusasthali, amidst the beauties of Raivataka Mountain. We have constructed such fortresses there that, living within their safety, even a battalion of women can easily fight an invading army, not to speak of brave warriors of the Brishni lineage. Oh King, at present we are settled in that township without any fear.... The mountain on which we have built our home is three *yojanas*[2] in length and more than one *yojana* in width. It has twenty-one peaks."

In my opinion what is said in the above portion of the *Mahabharata* bears the marks of authenticity as, from the point of style, it appears to have come directly from the original version of that book[3]. And as I have explained to my readers earlier the original *Mahabharata* is much older than *Harivansha* or the *Puranas*. If that is so then we have to accept that Jarasandha's attacking Mathura eighteen times and being pushed back on each occasion is only a made up story. Possibly there was a tentative attempt by Jarasandha to take Mathura and before he could make a second attempt the Yadavas had abandoned it to build their colony on

---

[2] *Translator's Footnote*
One *Yojana* = 4 *Kroshas* or 12.8 kilometres
[3] *Translator's Footnote*
Bankim uses two terms frequently (a) original *Mahabharata* (b) *Mahabharata*.
It is important therefore to be clear about what he means by those two terms. According to Bankim the original *Mahabharata* is the very first version of the story, which bears the signs of being the work of a single author. It was a short and simple narrative told probably around 1400 BC.
What Bankim calls the *Mahabharata* is how we find the epic today. With this version he sometimes uses the adjectives 'current' or 'prevalent'. This is at least four times longer than the original work and bears the signs of being extended over a long period of time with contributions from many authors.

the hills from where they could defend themselves better against any more possible invasions by the tyrant. After this move by the Yadavas Jarasandha, probably, did not consider it worth his might to try to subdue them.

Whatever it may be, what we come to know about Krishna from his approach to the threat of Jarasandha is that (along with the other leaders of his clan) he was an able statesman and strategist and so he tried to avoid unnecessary conflicts and loss of lives.

◆

Life in Dwaraka

Krishna was not the king of Dwaraka. As far as we can make out, the Yadavas ruled themselves by the system of oligarchy. That is, they had several equally powerful leaders among them. We also find that within the system, the elders were usually given more respect than the other leaders. It was only for this reason that Ugrasena had the title of King. In reality, leadership rested upon the person who excelled in intellectual as well as physical endowments. This is the reason why Krishna was accepted as the leader of the clan. Even his elder brother Balarama and others like Kritavarma – who were older to Krishna – listened to his advice and followed him. On his part, Krishna was always concerned about his people's well-being. Whenever Krishna gained any asset by any conquest, he shared it with his relatives. He was equally kind to every one of them.

However, as generally happens within a community, a few people were jealous of Krishna's position. There is a passage in the *Mahabharata* where Krishna describes the situation himself. I cannot say for sure if this passage is authentic but am presenting it to my readers as it is an interesting commentary on community psychology:

Bhishma relates to Yudhisthira what Narada said he (Narada) had heard from Krishna, "Have given half of my wealth to my relatives and yet I live as if I am their servant and am criticised over and over again. I have powerful supporters like Balarama and Pradyumna… and yet feel helpless. I have two wonderful friends in Ahuka and Akrura but as soon as I show a little affection to one of them, the other gets angry with me. Have, therefore, stopped showing love to either of them. I am having great trouble in keeping peace with these two friends."

Sri Krishna's Consorts

Krishna's first wife was Rukmini. She was the daughter of Bhismaka, the ruler of Vidharva. It is said that charmed by the description of Rukmini's accomplishments and beauty, Krishna had approached Bhismaka and begged for his daughter's hand. Rukmini, too, was attracted to Krishna.

However, on the advice of Jarasandha, Krishna's famous enemy, Bhismaka refused to give Rukmini's hand to Krishna. Worse, he arranged her marriage to Shishupala, the Krishna-hater. Fixing the date for the wedding, he invited all the neighbouring rulers except, of course, the Yadavas.

Krishna decided to visit Bhismaka's kingdom uninvited. And, with the help of his Yadava friends, he planned to abduct Rukmini.

It is popularly believed that, on the day fixed for her wedding with Shishupala, Krishna lifted Rukmini on his chariot while she was coming out of a shrine. Bhismaka, his sons, Jarasandha, and other rulers on their side were prepared for such an eventuality as they had heard of Krishna's arrival in town. All of them chased Krishna, but in vain. Nobody could overtake him or the other Yadavas. Krishna took Rukmini to Dwaraka, where he married her according to the sacred rituals.

In Krishna's time, the above method of marriage was called *harana* or capturing the bride. This method, we must note, did not indicate that the girls taken to be brides were tortured in any way. Especially, if the girl was willing to marry her abductor, how could we blame him? In the case of Rukmini and Krishna, both were attracted to each other.

Later, we will see how even the capturing of Subhadra by Arjuna with the approval of Krishna was neither a mistake nor an act of cruelty.

However, before taking such a bold stand on this matter, we have to successfully defend our approach. In our case, this has been done by Krishna himself in the context of Subhadra's marriage with Arjuna to which we will come shortly.

In those days, *Kshatriyas* generally married in either of these methods – *swayamvara* or *harana*. On some occasions, both the methods operated together. For example, Bhishma, the ideal *Kshatriya* bachelor, came to the *swayamvara sabha* of Kashi Raja's daughters as one of the guests, but committed *harana* of Amba, Ambika and Ambalika to make them the brides of his younger half-brothers.

Because, the *Kshatriyas* were hot-tempered people, there used to be frequent rivalries among their young men over prospective brides. When someone won a lady through *swayamvara* or through *harana*, his jealous rivals would be up in arms. Sometimes, a battle would start even before a lady had been won over.

In the *Mahabharata* however – in the portions which appear to have come from the original version of the book – we do not find any mention of Rukmini being captured by *harana*, though there is some reference of a kind of conflict taking place when Rukmini was married to Krishna.

Reference to Rukmini's *harana* appears in the 157th section of *Udyoga Parva* in the *Mahabharata*. There is reason to believe, however, that that section of the *Mahabharata* was interpolated later and is not a part of the original version.

Following is the premise of my coming to that conclusion:

Currently the chapter in the *Mahabharata* that is called *Udyoga Parva* has 197 sections. However, as I have mentioned before, in the introduction of the *Mahabharata* where the gist of the chapters are given, there is a mention of only 186 sections in *Udyoga Parva*. Thus, 11 of the sections are definitely interpolated. Considering the style and the contents of 157th section of *Udyoga Parva*, I feel that it is one of the 11 sections added later.

Ultimately, however, it hardly matters whether Rukmini was abducted by Krishna or not as *harana* was an accepted nuptial procedure in his time.

An Odd Legend about Sri Krishna's Consorts

According to a popular legend, Earth had a son called Narakasura. He ruled Pragjyotisha. Troubled by his destructive activities, Lord Indra himself came to Dwaraka, met Krishna and complained to him about the troublemaker. Among other abominable acts, Narakasura had stolen the *Kundala* of Aditi, the mother of the gods. Krishna promised Indra that he would destroy Narakasura and kept his promise by slaying him in Pragjyotishapura. Narakasura had sixteen thousand daughters. Krishna married all of them!

Satyabhama

Satrajita, a Jadava, had acquired a very attractive gem called *Samantaka*. When Krishna saw that gem he felt it was only fit for their king Ugrasena. So Satrajita feared that Krishna would take away the gem from him. To hide it from Krishna, he gave the gem to his brother Prosena to wear. However, Prosena was killed in the forest and the gem was lost. The citizens of Dwaraka suspected Krishna of stealing the gem.

Desperate to prove his innocence, Krishna went out in search of the gem and somehow found it with a woman who lived in the area where Prosena was attacked by a lion. Krishna returned the gem to Satrajita. Pleased, and to be in the good books of Krishna, Satrajita offered his daughter Satyabhama to him in marriage. Satyabhama was a beautiful and accomplished girl and her other suitors were disappointed that she was married away.

In *Harivansha*, it is said that Satrajita had three daughters and all three were offered to Krishna.

In popular folklore, it is believed that Sri Krishna had more than sixteen thousand wives! However, the several lists of Krishna's wives given in *Harivansha*, *Vishnu Purana* and even in the *Mahabharata* do not tally with one another. Different names are given in different places and the total number of wives vary from list to list.

To my mind, sufficient material can be extracted from various texts to support the premise that Krishna had only one wife, Rukmini. We find that Satyabhama's son Shuni is not given any importance anywhere, while Rukmini's descendant becomes the future king. The tracts in the *Mahabharata* where Satyabhama is mentioned seem to me to be later additions. For example, Satyabhama is said to accompany Krishna to

Upaplavya city where Krishna comes after he had formally embraced the Pandava's side in the impending Kurukshetra war (that is, he comes prepared for a war, in which he has soon to participate, albeit unarmed). It seems unlikely to me that he would bring his wife along on such a trip.

In conclusion, it is quite possible, though, that Krishna had several wives. Polygamy was a prevalent social practice in his time and he might have followed the custom.

◆

Section - IV
Indraprastha

Draupadi's Swayamvara

In the *Mahabharata*, Krishna appears for the first time at Draupadi's *swayamvara sabha*. We have reasons to believe that this part comes from the original *Mahabharata*. I do not suppose, however, that Draupadi was born out of sacrificial fire or that she had five husbands. But it is possible that Draupadi was king Dhrupad's biological daughter. It is also possible that in her *swayamvara sabha*, Arjuna had won her by accomplishing a difficult teat of archery. Whether she had five husbands after that or only one is open to controversy. Anyway, in the introduction of the original *Mahabharata* – where Vyasa gives a gist of the epic in 150 *slokas* – he does not say that Draupadi had five husbands.

As I said, in the *Mahabharata*, we find Krishna for the first time at Draupadi's *swayamvara*. Here we find him as a human being, not as a god. Along with other *Kshatriyas*, the Yadavas were invited for the *swayamvara* and a group of them had come to Panchala to attend the ceremony. However, we do not find any of the Yadavas taking part in the archery contest.

The Pandava brothers were present in the gathering, incognito. They were on the move from place to place in disguise as they knew that Duryodhana wanted to assassinate them. (The Kauravas actually believed them already dead, burnt by Purochana in Varanavata).

Hearing of the function of a *swayamvara* in king Dhrupad's kingdom, the Pandavas joined in. Among the *Brahmins* and *Kshatriyas* assembled there, it was Krishna alone who recognised them. Krishna could do this, not because he was superhuman, but because he was exceptionally intelligent. (Moreover, Sri Krishna's spies had told him earlier that the Pandavas had not died in the fire in Varanavata).

Krishna shared what he had guessed with Baladeva thus, "Sir, the person who is drawing the immense bow is Arjuna. I have no doubt about that. And the person who has uprooted a tree before entering the assembly hall is Brikodara (another name of Bhima)."

Later, when Krishna met Yudhisthira and was asked, "How did you recognise us?", Krishna had replied, "Can fire be hidden beneath ash?"

It was surely difficult to see through the Pandavas' disguise. That Sri Krishna gauged the truth indicates his sharpness of mind and his ability to think fast.

The *Mahabharata* does not explicitly say this but what we find in its pages is that Krishna was only a human being, but probably, the wisest and the brightest human being of his time.

Arjuna proved himself to be the most accomplished archer in the assembly as only his arrow could penetrate the mark. (He had to pierce the eye of a revolving fish hung high above him taking aim only by its reflection in the water at ground level). This agitated the other noblemen present there. "How dare a begging Brahmin (Arjuna was wearing the costume of a Brahmin) win a princess!" they thought, and attacked him. At this, Krishna came forward as a peacemaker and was able to prevent a crisis.

In the *Mahabharata*, this is the first time that we find Krishna engaged in a good cause. How he brought peace in this particular occasion throws much light on his character. There were several ways of averting the crisis. For example, a brave and able warrior, Sri Krishna could have taken up arms on behalf of Arjuna (his cousin on his mother's side) and could have defeated the enemy with the help of his supporters Baladeva and Satyaki. Bhima, for example, did not hesitate in taking up arms on that occasion. But an ideal *Dharmik* (one who does the right thing always), he would not be aggressive where peaceful means could work. He had no objection to war where it was the only means to uphold righteousness. In fact, in his opinion, not participating in such a war would be morally wrong.

So, he addressed the aggressing monarchs thus, "Oh, kings! These brothers have rightfully won the princess. Please calm down and stop fighting with them."

In those days, *Kshatriya* rulers were generally required to follow *Dharma* or righteousness. They thought that this would do them good. However, Arjuna's stunning feat and his winning of Draupadi had given them such a shock that they temporarily forgot their principles. Krishna brought them to their senses by reminding them of *Dharma*. The hostility stopped. The Pandavas returned to their *ashram*.

Now, it is obvious that if some insignificant and petty person had tried to calm down the enraged noblemen by reminding them of *Dharma*, he would not have been as successful as Sri Krishna had been. Krishna's ability to influence mighty rulers proves that he was already credited to be a trustworthy leader and had a commanding position in society.

Report of Krishna's Meeting with Yudhisthira

Arjuna returned to his *ashram* with his brothers after his victory at the *swayamvara*. The other nobles too returned to their respective places. There was no apparent reason for Krishna to stay on in Panchala. He could have returned to his own territory like the other invitees. However, he did not leave immediately. Taking Baladeva with him, he went to the abode where the Pandavas had put up. There he contacted Yudhisthira.

Personally, Krishna had nothing to gain from this visit. He had never met Yudhisthira before and they did not know each other. The author of the *Mahabharata* has written: "Vasudeva, coming to Yudhisthira touched his feet and introduced himself. Baladeva also did the same." This indicates that they had not known one another previously. This was the very first meeting of Krishna and the Pandavas. Krishna contacted the Pandavas only because they were his aunt Kunti's sons[4].

This was, surely, magnanimous on his part, for ordinarily people choose to interact only with rich and powerful relatives. The Pandavas, at that time, were poor.

---

[4] *Translator's Footnote*
Kunti never seems to have sought the help of her parental house, the Yadavas.... When her husband had died and she herself was placed in the lowly position of a dependant at the Kaurava household, Kunti could not expect anyone from her father's home to come and willingly share her own indignity. Certainly, she and her fatherless children would have found a home with the Yadavas, but she feared that their absence from Hastinapura would endanger their claim to the throne. Even today, a wise widow would thus live humbly in her brother-in-law's house so as not to jeopardise her son's right to the ancestral property. *(Source: Irawati Karve)*

Krishna stayed on in Panchala to attend Draupadi's wedding with the Pandavas. As wedding gift from him, he sent them jewellery, clothes, bedding, household utility goods, elephants and horses, along with other valuables. Thereafter, Krishna left Panchala without meeting the Pandavas.

The above conduct of Krishna was a tiny act of kindness but it reveals that he was large-hearted.

The Harana of Subhadra

Next we meet Sri Krishna at the *harana* of Subhadra. What he did in connection to that *harana* would have been totally disapproved by the 19th century society. (*Harana* is capturing a girl to marry her. A *Rakshasa* wedding is a wedding where the groom captures the bride by *harana*). However, behind the social laws of countries, there is a universal law of human behaviour – independent of space and time. And here, let us judge Krishna's actions by that universal, unchangeable law.

But, before beginning to analyse Krishna's merit or demerit in this episode, let us see if the episode itself is part of the fundamental *Mahabharata*.

I have to admit that Subhadra's *harana*, which Krishna supports, is indeed part of the original version of the *Mahabharata*. The introduction as well as the gist of the epic refers to this incident. The poetry in the episode resembles that of the earliest *Mahabharata*. More importantly, if we delete this part from the *Mahabharata*, the epic itself will remain incomplete. Subhadra is the mother of Abhimanyu whose son Parikshita was the father of Janamejaya. Parikshita and Janamejaya ruled Hastinapura for more than a century. It was Subhadra's and not Draupadi's grandchildren who inherited the throne. Maybe we can delete Draupadi's *swayamvara* from the *Mahabharata* but we cannot delete Subhadra's *harana*.

Now, before I enter into the analysis of the social and moral implications of Subhadra's *harana*, I have a request for my readers.

Please forget what you have heard or read of this episode from popular literature. In those sensational tracts, Subhadra falls madly in love with Arjuna as soon as she sees him. Satyabhama brings this message to Arjuna who lifts Subhadra in his *Ratha* and flies through the airway.

That is not what had exactly happened. While the Pandavas were peacefully settled in Indraprastha after their marriage with Draupadi, Arjuna, for some reason, was away from home for twelve years when he visited many places. One of the places he went to was Dwaraka. The Yadavas welcomed him. Arjuna stayed in Dwaraka for a while. Once, while he was there, the citizens of Dwaraka, including young men and girls had a grand feast on Raivataka hills. Subhadra was present there with other maidens. She was young and yet unmarried. Arjuna was charmed by her.

Krishna teased him, "Even while roaming in the forests you get stricken by love?" Arjuna admitted his weakness but sought his friend's advice as to how he could make Subhadra his bride. Krishna advised him thus, "Dear Arjuna, for getting a bride, *swayamvara* is a respectable procedure for a *Kshatriya*. However, you cannot predict a woman's choice in a *swayamvara*. I am afraid, therefore, you cannot depend on that method. On the other hand, according to the *Dharmashastras*, it is also prestigious for a *Kshatriya* to abduct a lady and marry her. Win my sister by force. Who knows whom she will choose otherwise!"

Resolving to act on that advice, Arjuna sent a messenger to bring Yudhisthira's and Kunti's approval for the match. On receiving their blessings, he captured Subhadra one day while she was returning to Dwaraka from the Raivataka hills and departed with her in his chariot.

It is obvious that in today's world Arjuna's conduct would not only be shameful but also punishable. And a person who advises his friend to steal his sister would be severely criticised too. However, this incident happened four thousand years ago. Let us see what the systems of marriage at that time were.

The scripture *Manu Samhita* recommends eight types of wedding:

1. Brahma wedding 2. Deyva wedding 3. Arya wedding 4. Prajapati wedding 5. Asura wedding 6. Gandharva wedding 7. Rakshasa wedding 8. Paishacha wedding

Of these eight types of wedding, the *Kshatriya* had the right to the last four. Of these four, *Paishacha* and *Asura* weddings were not encouraged for anybody. Thus, only *Gandharva* and *Rakshasa* weddings were left for a respectable *Kshatriya*.

Gandharva marriage can take place where the bride and groom love each other. In this case, Subhadra's sentiments were unknown. Therefore, for Arjuna, *Rakshasa* wedding was the only course open which the then society would readily approve.

Now, people may ask me, "You suggest that Manu approved of *Rakshasa* wedding, but where is the proof that *Manu Samhita* existed when Subhadra's *harana* took place?"

It is true that we cannot say for sure that *Manu Samhita* had been put together or had taken shape prior to Arjuna and Subhadra's marriage. However, it is accepted by scholars that that book is nothing but a record of social conventions prevalent in the years preceding its inception. If that is so, it would not be incorrect to assume that *Rakshasa* wedding was a common practice among the *Kshatriyas* during Yudhisthira's reign.

Besides, the narration of the *Mahabharata* itself refers to the fact that *harana* was accepted by society. In this same context of Subhadra-Arjuna's alliance, Krishna had to express his personal opinion about it from the position of a trustworthy leader of his community.

It happened in the following way:

On Arjuna's abduction of Subhadra, the Yadavas were deeply upset and angry. They started preparations for attacking Arjuna. At this point Baladeva said, "Before engaging ourselves in a conflict let us see what Krishna has to say about the matter. I find that he has kept quiet."

Addressing Krishna, Baladeva expressed his wrath against Arjuna for bringing dishonour to their family (*kula*). He then wanted to know what Krishna thought would be the right course of action for the Yadavas under the circumstances.

Krishna replied, "Arjuna has not brought dishonour to our family. In fact, he has added to its honour. Arjuna did not belittle us by offering us money for Subhadra's hand. He knows we are not greedy. It is extremely difficult to win one's chosen girl in a *swayamvara*. So Arjuna couldn't depend on that system. And for a mighty *Kshatriya* like him, it would not be praiseworthy to beg a girl's hand from her parents. I am sure, our cousin Arjuna, after reflecting upon the pros and cons of the ways open to him of winning Subhadra, has taken recourse to *harana*. I find this alliance totally acceptable for our family. Moreover, it confers glory on Subhadra as the person who has won her by force is of high birth and excels in learning and intellect."

I trust my readers would not conclude that I personally approve of *Rakshasa* wedding. It is unnecessary to waste words in saying how severely it should be denounced. That it was acceptable and upheld in those ancient times is not Krishna's fault.

Many among us believe that only a reformer can be an ideal human being. So they might argue that if Sri Krishna was an ideal human being he needed to be a reformer, he needed to take action against social ills like *Rakshasa* weddings. But as we do not agree with the premise that only a reformer can be our hero, we cannot debate on this point of view. (Sri Krishna was not a reformer in the sense that he did not formulate novel ideas about how a society should be run. His goal in life was to uplift human communities only by reinstating *Dharma* wherever it had degenerated. The conception of *Dharma* itself was already an ancient idea.)

In the beginning of this chapter, I said that behind social laws of different countries, there is a universal law of human behaviour independent of space and time. Let us now analyse the implications of Subhadra's *harana* in the light of this universal law:

To get a bride by force can be denounced for three reasons:

- It can be harmful for the bride.
- It can be harmful for the bride's family.
- It can be harmful for the society at large.

In Subhadra's *harana*, since Arjuna was a capable and noble person, the bride would only benefit from the alliance. So it was not harmful for the bride.

About the family being adversely affected – the Yadavas had no reason to fear. We have seen how Krishna, the best among the Yadavas, explained how it would bring glory to them. Realising their mistake, the seething Yadavas calmed down, and after some reflection on the matter, brought Arjuna and Subhadra back and gave them a ceremonial wedding.

Thirdly, regarding the society at large, it is clear that Arjuna had not harmed it by abducting his bride as such application of force was sanctioned by the norms of his time. That is, the act did not make Arjuna an outlaw.

There is a reason why I write about the above matter so elaborately. We have a tendency at present to judge everything by yardsticks that we have borrowed from the West. However, to understand our ancient culture well, we have to occasionally relax those fixed Western yardsticks.

Fire in the Khandava Forest

In the *Mahabharata*, we meet Krishna next when he, accompanied by Arjuna, burns the Khandava forest, a forest near the Pandavas' kingdom in Khandavaprastha.

When we examine the stories that are in circulation about this undertaking we can easily make out that many of them are made up. In one story, for example, King Svetaki, who was a great performer of *Yajnas*, put so much strain on *Agni*, the fire that fuelled his *Yajnas*, that *Agni* fell ill. Brahma advised *Agni* to devour the Khandava forest to recover from his illness. As *Agni* started his meal by lighting the forest up, the inhabitants in it quenched the fire. Every time *Agni* started to eat the forest, the same thing happened. Desperate, disguised as a Brahmin, he came to Krishna and Arjuna, and begged them to burn the Khandava for him. So the two friends, armed with their arsenals, started in earnest to burn the forest. Indra showered rain on the fire but Arjuna's arrows quenched the rain. Other gods joined Indra in fighting Krishna and Arjuna but an oracle prevented the gods, for it announced that Krishna and Arjuna were ancient *rishis*.

For a storyteller, an oracle is a very convenient tool, for with it, a message can be broadcast without anybody having to own it. On this occasion, the gods disappeared after the oracle and the two friends continued to burn the forest without any resistance. The animals and the birds of the forest were all killed. *Agni*, cured of his illness, blessed Krishna and Arjuna, as did the defeated gods.

Now, the only facts that can be extracted from the above story is that there was a forest close to the Pandavas' kingdom with many animals and birds in it, which Krishna and Arjuna burned to annex the land to the Pandava holdings. If indeed that was the case, it is only a common practice for people needing more land. The inhabitants of Sundarbans do this every day. It indicates neither chivalry nor disgrace.

There are reasons why I discuss the burning of the Khandava in such detail. Firstly, even though the myths related here might be the work of third-category writers who added to the original *Mahabharata*, the main incident is probably true. Both the introduction and the summary of the *Mahabharata* contain this incident. Secondly, burning down the Khandava forest directly leads to *Sabha Parva*, which is one of the eighteen chapters of the *Mahabharata* recognised today. The construction of the *Sabha* and the *Rajasuya Yajna* performed there by the Pandavas are both very important events in moving the story of the *Mahabharata* forward.

Maya *Danava* is credited to have built the *Sabha* or conference hall mentioned above. He lived in the Khandava forest and was spared his life by Krishna and Arjuna when they burned the forest. He was an architect possessing special building skills. The suffix '*Danava*' to his name indicates that he was a non-Aryan.

Maybe Maya *Danava* is a fictitious character, but the poet who created him throws special light on Krishna's and Arjuna's characters when he describes his interactions with them.

As the story goes, grateful for being saved from the dreadful fire, Maya offered to repay Arjuna. But Arjuna would take nothing other than goodwill from him. At Maya's persistence with his offer, Arjuna replied, "Oh grateful one, you want to pay me for saving your life, but I do not have the heart for taking advantage of that." Yet, because Maya would be pleased only if allowed to be of service, Arjuna added, "However, I do not want to disappoint you. Please do something for Krishna. It would be doing something for me."

Krishna, too, refused to ask anything for himself but he said he wanted something for Yudhisthira. Since Maya was a skilled builder, Krishna urged him to build a beautiful conference hall for Yudhisthira.

Now, even though this request for a hall for Yudhisthira was not directly for himself, it was related to Krishna's personal goals and desires. At that point of time, Krishna had two aims in life – to preach righteousness, and to establish a kingdom based on the principles of righteousness (that is, to bring righteousness into politics). His eagerness to get a *Sabha* for Yudhisthira is the first hint in the *Mahabharata* of his intention of establishing a righteous political system in the country.

In the last chapter (in the context of Subhadra's *harana*), I said that Krishna did not try to reform society. As we move along analysing his character, we find that instead of **reformation**, his aim was socio-political **regeneration**. He preached righteousness and tried to establish a political system based on righteousness. For him, the difference was like taking care of a branch of a tree (reformation) and taking care of the whole tree beginning from its roots (regeneration).

◆

Krishna, the Humanitarian

In this study of Krishna's character, I have discussed only his human qualities. What appear to be his superhuman qualities, I feel, are but exquisite refinements of his human qualities themselves. I do not contradict the idea that God can – for giving guidance to his people – take birth on earth. However, in such an incarnation, I believe, He would act only as a human being, performing only humanly possible activities. He would not demonstrate any superhuman power. This is because God, in His role of a human being, has to be a role-model for other human beings to follow. How can any ordinary person imitate a being who is supremely powerful?

In this context, let me quote from a sermon by Dr Brookly, delivered at Trinity Church, Boston on 29th March 1885: "We forget that Christ incarnate was such as we are, and some of us are putting him where he can be no example to us at all. Let no fear of losing the dear great truth of the divinity of Jesus make you lose the dear great truth of the humanity of Jesus. He took upon himself our nature; as a man of the like passions, he fought that terrible fight in the wilderness, year by year, as an innocent man, was he persecuted by narrow-hearted Jews; and his was a humanity whose virtue was pressed by all the needs of the multitude and yet kept his richness of nature; a humanity which, though given up to death to the cross, expressed all that is within the capacity of our own humanity; and if we really follow him we shall be holy even as he is holy."

I have the same thing to say about Sri Krishna. So even if we accept that Sri Krishna was divine, manifesting supernatural power would not be his goal. Whether in the story of the *Mahabharata*, the portions showing supernatural occurrences are later additions or not will be discussed later. At this moment, I would only say this: Krishna never tried to uphold himself as God and he tried to dissuade everybody from imposing godhood on him. He clearly admitted, "I can try my best to do whatever is humanly possible but I cannot perform anything by any divine power."

He carefully performed the rituals that were expected of him as a gentleman and a family man of his time. If he had any interest in proving himself to be divine, he would have done things differently to impress people. Contrarily, his leave-taking from the Pandavas – to go to Dwaraka after the burning of the Khandava forest – is full of common rituals, such rituals that a person without any claim to any special power would normally perform: "...His mind prepared for leave-taking, Krishna bathed and dressed himself and wore his ornaments. He then worshipped the gods and the Brahmins.... On reaching home, Vasudeva greeted his elderly father, his honourable mother and Ahuka.... Then taking permission from his elders, he entered Rukmini's quarters."

✦

Krishna's Advice to Kill Jarasandha

In Khandavaprastha, Yudhisthira's conference hall was ready. It was proposed by family and friends including *rishis* like Dhaumya and Dvaipayana that Yudhisthira must perform the *Rajasuya Yajna* there. But Yudhisthira would not undertake that huge task without Krishna's advice. So he sent for Krishna who came over immediately.

Addressing Krishna, Yudhisthira said, "I desire to perform the *Rajasuya Yajna*.... My friends too are advising me to undertake it. But I want to hear your opinion about the matter, Krishna!"

Yudhisthira knew that Krishna would be unflattering and totally honest and he was right. However gently, Krishna placed before him the bitter truth – that he was unfit for performing the *Yajna* as only an emperor had the capacity to do that. At that time, Jarasandha had a commanding position over the entire country and so he, not Yudhisthira, was the emperor in real sense of the term.

Jarasandha was also a wicked tyrant who had captured many less important rulers and had imprisoned them intending to slaughter them as human sacrifice before Lord Shiva. He was waiting just to collect a few more kings to complete the number he aimed for his ritualistic offering to Mahadeva.

"Oh light of the Bharata clan," Krishna addressed Yudhisthira, "...I suggest you fight Jarasandha and defeat him... for only the one who thwarts his act of cruelty towards the innocent kings... can become the next emperor."

People who accuse Krishna of selfishness and intrigue may comment, "Well, well, this was a typical suggestion from a person seeking his own gain. He was putting in place a master-plan for getting rid of his old enemy, Jarasandha."

However, it can be strongly argued that Krishna was, at that point of time, genuinely interested in doing away with Jarasandha for the sake of the release of the imprisoned kings and saving the land and its people from Jarasandha's tyranny. For, at that time, Krishna and his people were safely out of Jarasandha's harmful reach having established themselves on the fortress-like Raivataka hills.

In any case, even people who still insist that Krishna was manipulating the fall of Jarasandha for his own advantage have to admit that the removal of the tyrant also meant a greater good to a larger number of people. It would actually have been cowardly of Krishna if he had decided not to pursue his plan against Jarasandha just to protect his own reputation.

Yudhisthira, though himself hesitant of confronting Jarasandha, gave in to the enthusiasm of Bhima and Arjuna.

But it was almost impossible to defeat the tyrant's huge army. So, it was decided to invite Jarasandha for a duel fight with any of his three opponents – Bhima, Arjuna and Krishna – even though they were well aware that Jarasandha was no less a wrestler than any one of them. In those days, according to *Kshatriya Dharma*, a *Kshatriya* fighter was bound to respond to a challenge for a duel.

The three friends soon left for Jarasandha's kingdom.

Account of Krishna's Meeting with Jarasandha

In the *Mahabharata*, it is written that Krishna, Bhima and Arjuna met Jarasandha in disguise in the middle of the night. However, I find no real reason for the three of them to be in disguise as they revealed their identities readily to their opponent. It seems to me that their being in disguise was mentioned by some later poet just to add colour to the narrative. Krishna even referred to Jarasandha's dwelling as his enemy's house.

At this, Jarasandha wanted to know what was the enmity between them as he did not remember doing any harm to Krishna. Krishna could always conduct himself well and so he did not enter into a petty discussion on Jarasandha's invasions of the Yadavas. Knowing that at that point of time, he was only an agent of Yudhisthira engaged in clearing the ground for Yudhisthira's *Rajasuya*, Krishna said that Jarasandha was his enemy because he had imprisoned many dignified rulers. He added that Yudhisthira and his associates were righteous people who wanted to liberate the forcefully imprisoned kings in order to establish a righteous society and polity. Krishna declared that as Yudhisthira's representatives, the three of them had come to free the innocent rulers, if necessary, even by killing their prisoner.

Thus, we find that Krishna was ready to kill Jarasandha, if needed. Later, he would kill Shishupala. And we know that he had already killed Kansa. Now, the question may arise, how can he be an ideal human being even after taking so many lives? Would not persuading the criminals to become good citizens benefit them as well as the whole society? Why did not Sri Krishna do that?

There are two answers to this question:

Firstly, Krishna did try to make people understand and do the right and the kindly things. For example, he tried his best to stop Duryodhana and Karna from becoming bitter enemies of the Pandavas. It was in reference to that effort that he had categorically stated that he had no supernatural power; that he merely tried his best to do the right thing. It was impossible for Krishna to do impossible things because he was only a human being. Krishna had no power to miraculously transform Jarasandha or other wrong doers.

Secondly, I must admit that Krishna did not try hard enough to deliver people from evil. Jesus Christ and the Buddha had done more of that in their respective lives. This is because Jesus and the Buddha had made the spreading of their message of goodwill the sole purpose of their lives. Krishna, on the other hand, wanted to become a supremely balanced human being.

Jesus Christ and the Buddha were very superior human beings engaged in the most refined of human endeavours. They rose above ordinary lives and by that means inspired their community to rise above evil.

Krishna, on the other hand, was a multifaceted but balanced character who lived the life of a normal but a very bright human being. He was down to earth and a man of the world. When duty demanded, he punished the wicked to protect the good.

✦

The Duel of Bhima and Jarasandha

Nowhere in the *Mahabharata*, so far, do we come across Krishna being addressed to as Vishnu. And so far we do not find Krishna using any superhuman power. However, from this point onward, we find him addressed or introduced to as Vishnu. We even find some people worshipping him as Vishnu and we find him occasionally using divine power. Thus, in this matter, there is a sharp divide in the former and the latter part of the *Mahabharata*.

If any of my readers argues that in the first chapters of the *Mahabharata*, Sri Krishna did not reveal his divinity simply because there was no need for it, while later the need arose, I would reply that that was definitely not the case. This is because many a time, in the later chapters, we find Krishna showing divinity without any reason at all. For example, after the episode of Jarasandha's death, when Sri Krishna was leaving the venue with Bhima and Arjuna in a chariot, he invoked Garuda who immediately came and perched on the dome of the vehicle. Here, there was no need for Garuda to come, for he just sat there. It seems that he came there just to prove Krishna's divine power. The paradox is that the trio who did not require any divine intervention to kill Jarasandha would require special power to travel on a chariot!

Earlier, it is written that Krishna did not fight Jarasandha because Mahadeva had ordered against it and yet we find that Jarasandha, of his own free will, elects Bhima and not Krishna to battle with from among the two brothers and Krishna.

I hope that my readers have no doubt, like me, that some changes were made here in the original story and that the purpose of these fabrications was simply to support the view that Sri Krishna was Lord Vishnu himself.

In the original *Mahabharata*, no connection between Krishna and Vishnu is made because there the character of Krishna is clearly revealed as a human character. When the text came into the hands of later Krishna worshippers, they perceived this omission as deplorable. So borrowing such material from sources that would serve their purpose, they interpolated them in the later versions of the *Mahabharata*.

So the grateful rulers, when liberated from Jarasandha's clutches, addressed Krishna as 'Vishnu' even though Krishna had never before been addressed by that name or by any other name belonging to Vishnu. He had not even done anything remarkable about killing Jarasandha, even though it was he who had conceived the idea of killing him. Bhima was the one who had killed the tyrant. Indeed, the imprisoned rulers could not even have immediately known what role Krishna had in their liberation.

On the whole, according to my investigations, I find that the author of the original *Mahabharata* avoided sensationalism whereas the later poets brought in too much of it by describing miraculous happenings at random. A peculiar tract of description by a later poet is a sample of how they had exaggerated on realities:

"The vigorous and powerful Jarasandha living in a mountain range, swirled round a large mace 99 times and hurled it to kill Krishna. The mace reached Mathura and fell exactly 99 *yojanas* from where Krishna was busy at his work."

Let me conclude this chapter by referring to a few more details about the events surrounding Jarasandha's death. They reflect both the conventions of the time and on Krishna's character:

On selecting Bhima for fighting his duel, Jarasandha ritually prepared himself for the event under the guidance of a *Brahmin*. As required, he removed his armour and headgear. All the citizens of the locality, the *Brahmins*, the *Kshatriyas*, the *Vaishyas*, the *Shudras*, the fallen and the elderly gathered to watch the combat. The encounter went on for 14 days (probably including rest periods). On the 14th day, on finding Jarasandha tired, Krishna urged Bhima not to torture him. He said it was wrong to punish a tired rival. He suggested that Bhima should only fight with his hands.

However, Bhima still killed Jarasandha by unduly torturing him. His knowledge of *Dharma* and his loyalty to it were indeed less than those of Krishna.

After Jarasandha's death, Krishna, Arjuna and Bhima set the imprisoned rulers free. Then, they left the place. They were not annexationists. They would not punish a son for his father's misdeeds. So, Jarasandha's son Sahadeva became the next ruler of the kingdom.

The liberated royals, full of gratitude, wanted to be of service to Krishna and his team. Krishna asked them to help Yudhisthira to successfully conduct the *Rajasuya Yajna*. For, at that time, Krishna's goal in life was to build a righteous kingdom with Yudhisthira at its centre.

The Ritual of Honouring the Best Person in the Assembly

The *Rajasuya Yajna* of Yudhisthira commenced. The kingdom filled up with spectators from far and near. Kings, *rishis* as well as people of many other categories came. For the successful completion of the huge function, the Pandavas delegated responsibilities to their kinfolks. Dushasana was supervising food and meals, Sanjay was at hospitality, Kripacharya was the treasurer and the giver of alms, Duryodhana was in charge of gifts received. Sri Krishna is listed as voluntarily engaged in washing the feet of the Brahmins. I must admit that I do not understand why this was the case. Why was Sri Krishna occupied with such a petty job? Wasn't there a more important work that would suit him? Was bathing the *Brahmins'* feet considered in his time to be such a superior activity that only a very important person should do it for a *Yajna*? To prove himself an ideal human being, would he have to rinse even the feet of *Brahmins* employed in the kingdom as cooks?

Several explanations can be given as to why Sri Krishna undertook that lowly job. Firstly, the explanation proposed by the *Brahmins* themselves and readily accepted today, is that he wanted to demonstrate the glory of the *Brahmins*.

I do not think this is an acceptable explanation. For, even though it is true that Sri Krishna – like the other *Kshatriyas* of his time – gave due respect to the *Brahmins*, we never find him making any special effort to broadcast their glory. In fact, occasionally, we find him doing just the opposite. As an example, let us take the story (supposing it is true) in Vanaprastha where Sri Krishna tricks off Durbhasha, the *Brahmin* sage and his entourage from imposing upon the Pandavas' hospitality.

Krishna upheld the equality of all beings. If the message of the *Gita* is taken as Krishna's own message then we must believe that he considered the Brahmin, the cow, the elephant, the dog and the *Chandala* as equals. If that was his genuine opinion then I am sure he was not exceptionally keen on washing the *Brahmins'* feet to uphold the glory of that caste.

The second explanation is that because Krishna was an ideal human being, his humility was also ideal and so he had voluntarily accepted that humble job. Here, my question is why did he wash only the *Brahmins'* feet? Why not the feet of the elderly *Kshatriyas*? And, I have to say, also, that I do not call this type of humility ideal. This can only be the pretence of humility.

According to the third explanation, Krishna was attuned with his time. So, because in his time, *Brahmins* were excessively respected, bathing their feet was a strategic move on his part, by which he expected to gain popularity.

To me, though, the verse describing Sri Krishna's ablutions of the *Brahmins'* feet is a later addition to the original story. I say this because elsewhere in the same chapter, we find him occupied with another brave and responsible assignment. It is written there that holding his conch shell, his discus and his mace, Sri Krishna was on duty protecting the *Yajna* from start to finish.

In that *Yajna* of Yudhisthira, Krishna killed mighty Shishupala. This was one of the rare occasions when Krishna had used arms on behalf of the Pandavas.

The section of the *Mahabharata* describing Shishupala's end holds a very important historical data – probably one of the most important historical data that is hidden in the *Mahabharata*. It is as follows:

Krishna, for the first time in the epic, is openly addressed here as a divine being by his contemporaries. Further, we find that Bhishma, an important leader of the Kuru clan, strongly supports that view.

So, if we believe this to be a genuine data, then we have to accept that even if Krishna was not credited with divinity in his earlier life, he was credited with it later on. We also find that at the time of Yudhisthira's *Rajasuya Yajna*, there were two factions of people divided on the issue of Krishna's divinity – one group believing him to be an incarnation of Vishnu while the other group opposing the idea. Bhishma and the Pandavas were the principal supporters of the former view, while Shishupala was a leader of the opposition.

The conflict which ended Shishupala's life arose when Bhishma and his friends wanted to confer a special public honour to Krishna at the commencement of Yudhisthira's *Rajasuya Yajna*. Shishupala objected to this as he thought Krishna was unworthy of such a prestigious decoration. A serious conflict arose in the gathering among Krishna's supporters and his rivals, threatening to spoil the main ceremony. Krishna executed Shishupala to restore peace because he was in charge of protecting the main event.

We cannot be sure if this incident really happened. However, prior to the encounter in context, there is a mention, in the *Mahabharata*, of a powerful ruler called Shishupala who is later absent. It can be assumed that he was killed in between. And because there is no information contradicting that Krishna had executed him, we might consider it to be true. Also, we should note that both the gist and the introduction of the *Mahabharata* carry this episode. Moreover, the literary style of this part of the narrative matches the beauty of the original *Mahabharata*. The dramatic presentation here, as in the original *Mahabharata*, is excellent. Let us now discuss in some detail the episode of Shishupala's end.

Even today in our country, the tradition of honouring the chief guest at any important function with sandalwood paste and a garland is observed. Today, however, the chief guest is often chosen not by his individual merit but by the status of his birth. In a house where everybody is of high caste, the eldest gets the honour. In Krishna's time, the custom differed slightly. In any assembly, the most meritorious individual used to get the honour, irrespective of his age and family connections.

Among Yudhisthira's guests, who would be the chosen one? Bhishma declared that Krishna was the greatest among the gathered noblemen as he most suitably met all the requirements of his caste (i.e. he was an ideal *Kshatriya*).

On Bhishma's advice, Krishna was anointed. And, Krishna acknowledged it by a formal and honourable retnal of acceptance.

Green with envy, Shishupala could not tolerate this. He delivered a long speech criticising Bhishma, Krishna and the Pandavas. In the beginning what he said was reasonable enough. Krishna was not the head of a state, he pointed out, so why honour him while many rulers themselves were present in the assembly? Was Krishna chosen because he was well established in society? Why was not his father Vasudeva chosen, then? Was Krishna selected because he was a relative and a well-wisher of the Pandavas? Why not their father-in-law Dhrupad, then? Was Krishna preferred because he was a good teacher (Krishna had given lessons on the technique of warfare to the famous warriors Abhimanyu and Satyaki and to several others including Arjuna)? Why select him instead of Dronacharya? Should Krishna be honoured because he had studied the Vedas well? (Thus, here is the admission that Krishna was a erudite Vedic scholar). But why place him over Veda Vyasa?

As generally happens with an orator, His Highness Shishupala got carried away by what he spoke. Forgetting logic, he began to utter whatever came to his head. Abandoning reasonable arguments, he began calling names, and following the laws of effective speech, he moved from less potent to more potent epithets. In describing Krishna from 'biased' and 'immature', he advanced to 'fallen from *Dharma*', 'wicked soul', 'impotent' and 'a dog'.

Krishna patiently listened to all that, even though he was powerful enough to vanquish his tormenter instantly. Even though he was not used to this kind of insult, he quietly excused Shishupala again and again.

Being the host of the ceremony, Yudhisthira tried to pacify the troublemaker with sweet words. But elderly Bhishma could not tolerate that. He said, "One who doesn't approve of Krishna's felicitation should neither be pleasantly spoken to nor shown any sympathy."

He, then, for the benefit of the assembly, began to enumerate the reasons for which he had recommended Krishna. I produce below the gist of what Bhishma said. But let me point out that there is something very strange in Bhishma's arguments. What is strange in them is that sometimes Bhishma praises Krishna as a good *Kshatriya* while at other times he praises him as God – the power behind the entire Universe. The discrepancy comes out very starkly in his speech and I urge my readers to draw their own conclusions about this dichotomy.

Bhishma said:

"In this assembly of aristocrats, there is nobody whom Krishna has not surpassed in strength and energy".

The statement describes Sri Krishna as he was as a human being. But immediately, thereafter, he is described as God:

"*Acchuta* is worshipped not only by us but also by the three worlds. The whole Universe reposes in Him."

Again, Sri Krishna's human identity is referred to:

"Since birth, Krishna has done great things. Over and over again I have heard people praising him and I keep on hearing about his many accomplishments."

Next, re-elevation to godliness:

"I have recommended the worship of *Acchuta* who is the harbinger of happiness and is adored by the whole world."

Earthliness, again, clearly stated:

"We have two reasons for choosing Krishna for today's honour. First, he is an authority on the *Vedas*. Second, he surpasses his peers in valour. Some of his additional qualities are his kindness, generosity, humility, politeness, sharpness of intellect, contentment and physical beauty."

Back to godliness immediately, thereafter:

"Krishna is the creator, preserver and destroyer of the Cosmos. He is Nature itself. He is timeless. He is the lord of every living thing. Krishna is the repository of the five elements of creation. The moon, the sun, the planets and the stars dwell in Krishna…"

Ultimately, of all that Bhishma said in praise of Krishna that day, two issues convincingly stand out to tell us how he was really superior to the others – firstly, his exceptional valour and secondly, his knowledge of the *Vedas*. When we study the story of Krishna's life, we come across many instances of his exceptional valour. His knowledge of the *Vedas* is reflected in the religion he preached in his *Gita*.

It is quite unlikely that what we read as *Bhagavat Gita* was actually written by Krishna. Also known as *Vyasiki Samhita*, it was probably written by Vyasa himself. Any way, the author of the *Gita*, whoever might he be, I imagine, had based his writing on what Krishna had believed and preached in his lifetime. Now, the point I want to make is that even though the *Gita* reveals that Krishna had not blindly accepted all that was said in the *Vedas*, but had criticised the *Vedas* bluntly from time to time, his own principle of *Dharma* was, nevertheless, inspired by Vedic literature. This would be clear to anybody who reads both the *Gita* and the *Vedas*. No doubt, therefore, that Krishna had studied the *Vedas* meticulously.

I personally call Sri Krishna an ideal human being because in analysing his character so far I found him to be knowledgeable, brave, accomplished, hardworking, dutiful, kind, forgiving and one who sincerely followed *Dharma* and the laws of society.

◆

The Slaying of Shishupala

Giving his reasons for choosing Krishna over all others for the special honour, Bhishma added that Shishupala could leave the assembly if its proceedings were not to his liking.

Shishupala's eyes widened with anger and he began to tremble. In this condition, he approached the other dignitaries and urged them to take his side. He said he had worked as a commander of an army before and with that experience, if the noblemen were ready to assist him, he would immediately stop Yudhisthira's coronation and Krishna's felicitation.

Realising that the gathering was turning hostile, Yudhisthira sought Bhishma's guidance which brought another spate of name-calling from Shishupala. He called Krishna 'wicked', 'someone whom even kids hate', 'a cow keeper' and 'a servant'.

Bhishma commanded him to keep quiet and reminded him that Krishna was the source of all his strength. This inflamed Shishupala's rage. He threatened that the gathered nobles, if they wanted to, could crush Bhishma in an instant. Bhishma retorted that he considered them as ineffectual as blades of grass.

This provoked the committee of noblemen. A shout arose, "Kill Bhishma like an animal or burn him alive!"

Ultimately reason prevailed on Bhishma's suggesting that as Krishna's eligibility for a special honour was the matter of contention, Krishna himself should be called upon to prove his superiority.

Shishupala immediately agreed and spent no time in inviting Krishna for a show down.

However, Krishna was not in a hurry even though as a *Kshatriya* his natural preference would have been to respond to that battle-call immediately. Krishna was especially composed and careful on that occasion as he was protecting Yudhisthira's *Yajna* and was very keen on fulfilling his duty well.

He addressed the assembly and calmly explained his reasons for the move he would soon be taking. He revealed that many times in the past he had tolerated the worries and the losses Shishupala had caused him (Shishupala once had set fire to Dwaraka. Once he had killed and captured many Yadavas. He had stolen Krishna's father Vasudeva's *Ashwamedha* horse. These were some of the troubles he had caused to Krishna). But this time, he was unable to forgive him. In his speech, Krishna also mentioned that he had spared Shishupala again and again so far only on his aunt's, Shishupala's mother's request.

Is the story about the aunt a later addition? One cannot say for sure. However, I personally do not feel that the story is awkward or unnatural in any way. Aware of her son's hatred for the powerful Krishna, it would have been quite normal for the mother to make that request to Krishna. It is also understandable why Krishna raised the matter on that particular occasion. He wanted to publicly announce how he had honoured his aunt's trust for as long as he could.

Something unbelievable happened at that stage in the conference. Sri Krishna invoked his *Sudarshan* discus which magically came to his hand. He used it to cut off Shishupala's head. That this version of Shishupala's end is a later addition in the *Mahabharata* is obvious because elsewhere in the same book the episode is described in a different way. Bhishma related how Shishupala was killed in *Udyoga Parva*, where there was no mention of the *Chakra*. Krishna is shown fighting a humanly battle from a chariot.

Securing Yudhisthira's *Yajna* had made it necessary for Krishna to kill Shishupala.

Exile of the Pandavas

After the *Rajasuya Yajna*, Krishna returned to Dwaraka. We do not find him in the proceedings of the *Sabha Parva* (where Yudhisthira was defeated in a game of dice and lost even Draupadi whom Dushasana had tried to disrobe). However, Sri Krishna's name comes up once in this chapter when Draupadi, in her distress, remembered him as 'the favourite of the *gopis*'. I have commented upon this particular phrase earlier.

Soon the Pandavas left for the forest where they would spend twelve years serving their term as losers in the dice game and spend the required one year incognito in King Virata's palace.

While the Pandavas were in the forest, there is reference of Krishna coming in contact with them thrice. And, of course, he was present in the palace when, at the end of the Pandava's hiding, Virata's daughter Uttara's wedding with Arjuna's son Abhimanyu was solemnised.

Section - V
Upaplavya

Warriors Choose their Sides

The portion of the *Mahabharata* called *Udyoga Parva* deals with important discussions on the concepts of punishment and forgiveness, and of power and its effective use.

A society may treat its criminals in two different ways – by forgiving them or by punishing them. However, if all crimes were forgiven, society would collapse, whereas, if every crime was punished, human beings would be reduced to animals. So maintaining a balance between the use of force and the use of kindness has to be an important issue in communal matters. This issue is the subject of *Udyoga Parva*. And the person who conducts the debate on this issue is Sri Krishna. In this sense, Sri Krishna is the hero of this particular section of the *Mahabharata*.

In his actions, so far, we have found Sri Krishna sometimes using force and sometimes using forgiveness in the best ways possible (for example, we spot him excusing people who harmed him but punishing others who harmed communities). In *Udyoga Parva*, we are presented with his thoughts about the subject.

In today's civilised societies, we have legal systems to help us deal with matters of forgiveness and punishment. If somebody's property is stolen and needs to be recovered, we consult lawyers. But in an age lacking the advantage of a developed legal system, individuals would often have to take their own decisions.

In practice, we usually find that powerful people use force to solve their problems, while weaker people use forgiveness. However, how should someone who is powerful and yet gentle and kind act? Krishna had to deal with that complex question.

I trust my readers are aware that the Pandavas defeated by Shakuni in a game of dice were bound to hand over their kingdom to Duryodhana for twelve years, while they themselves spent that time in the forest. After twelve years in the forest, they were further required to spend one year, anywhere, in disguise. If, within that one year, anybody could recognise them, they were bound to spend another twelve years in the forest.

However, if they managed to remain undiscovered in that thirteenth year, they were supposed to get their kingdom back. At this point of our discussion, the Pandavas had fulfilled both their obligations. By law and by *Dharma*, they had the right to their kingdom. But would Duryodhana give it back to them? Possibly not. In that case, wasn't it fair enough for the Pandavas to fight for its recovery?

At the end of their year in disguise in King Virata's palace, the Pandavas revealed their identities to their host. Overjoyed, Virata proposed his daughter Uttara's marriage to Arjuna's son Abhimanyu. To participate in the solemn ceremony, relatives and well-wishers from far and near came. Krishna and Baladeva, the maternal uncles of Abhimanyu, were there. The Pandavas' father-in-law Dhrupad was also there as were other guests related by marriage to the Pandavas.

In the course of time, the wedding guests in Virata's palace raised the topic of what the Pandavas should do to recover their rightful provinces from Duryodhana, in case he did not give them back to the Pandavas on his own. Soon, they were all looking up at Sri Krishna for guidance. Sri Krishna, now, had to conduct the meeting. He began by addressing the party and describing the situation in all its details for everybody's benefit.

Then he urged them to think of a solution that would be in the best interests of the Pandavas as well as the Kauravas and would be dignified and according to *Dharma*. He himself was even ready for compromise and totally approved of a proposal by Yudhisthira that only half of what was due to the Pandavas would satisfy them. His advice was that a *Dharmika* gentleman should approach Duryodhana with Yudhisthira's message of compromise and peace.

We notice that Krishna was not just pleading for the recovery of the Pandavas' land. He was pleading for righteousness to prevail. The gain or loss of one individual was not the issue here. The issue was that someone was being cheated and that needed to be stopped to safeguard the principles on which society depended. Personally, Krishna preferred peaceful means of settling differences over any kind of aggression. And later, when war was unavoidable, Sri Krishna abstained from taking up arms.

In Virata's assembly, after Krishna's speech, Baladeva took his turn. He supported what Krishna had said. And, he blamed Yudhisthira for choosing to play the game of dice, in the first place.

As if in a parliamentary procedure, another important dignitary in the assembly rose up next. He was Satyaki. A disciple of Krishna, he was sturdy and brave. We find his praises later in the *Mahabharata* as a warrior on the Pandava side in greatness next only to Arjuna and Abhimanyu. Satyaki said he did not favour any peace treaty or compromise. If the Kauravas did not return the Pandavas' property in full, the Kauravas should be destroyed. Taking turn to express his opinion, elderly Dhrupad supported Satyaki. He further advised that the Pandavas should begin to contact friends for the purpose of accumulating soldiers. At the same time, however, he wanted to send a messenger to Duryodhana to negotiate peace.

At the end of the conference, Krishna spoke again. As before, he appealed for peace. And he announced that in case war was inevitable, he intended not to take any combative part in it. The Kauravas were related to him as closely as the Pandavas were and they had always been respectful to him. Therefore, he did not want to take sides. However, if Duryodhana did not accept Yudhisthira's terms for a peace treaty and war became a necessity, he realised that he had no choice but to be a part of it. Still, he wanted to wait till the very last moment to take that step.

Soon, both the parties started to prepare for war. Representatives of both left for their respective friends to enrol them for active service. To embrace Krishna for the war Arjuna himself went to Dwaraka and so did Duryodhana. Both of them reached Krishna's residence on the same day at the same time. As the *Mahabharata* relates, Sri Krishna was asleep at that time. Entering his bedroom first Duryodhana took a chair near the head of the bed. Coming in next, Arjuna sat at Sri Krishna's feet, his hands joined in supplication. On waking up, Sri Krishna saw first Arjuna and then Duryodhana. Greeting both of them graciously, he enquired the reason for their visit.

Duryodhana smiled and said, "Oh, Yadava, please help me in the impending war! Even though you are related to Arjuna in the same way as you are with me and have similar goodwill for both of us, you have to take my side as honest people always entertain the first comer."

Krishna replied, "Oh brave Kaurava, I have no doubt in my mind that you arrived here first but I set my eyes on Arjuna before I saw you. I shall, therefore, help you both. It is customary to begin with the younger and so I shall speak to Arjuna first."

Addressing Arjuna, Sri Krishna said, " Oh son of Kunti, I shall respond to your appeal for help. There is a special unit of our army consisting of 100 million soldiers of the Gopa sub-caste, each member as strong a warrior as myself. That unit can join one side while I join the other as a non-fighting assistant. Now, Arjuna, make your choice."

Well knowing that Sri Krishna would be without weapons, Arjuna still chose him over his *Narayani Sena*. Duryodhana was thrilled to have the soldiers instead.

When we analyse this far of *Udyoga Parva*, we find the following important facts about Krishna:

Even though Krishna rightly felt that it was a person's duty to protect his own property, he considered forgiveness and sacrifice superior to aggression. He readily approved of Yudhisthira's bid of giving away half of his kingdom for the sake of peace.

Krishna was impartial. It is commonly believed that Krishna supported the Pandavas against the Kauravas. But we find here that he did not want to take sides.

In spite of being a great warrior himself, Krishna detested wars and was reluctant to take part in any. Till the last minute, he endeavoured to stall the war of Kurukshetra. And when it was inevitable, he abstained from taking up arms himself. We do not find such greatness in any other *Kshatriya*, including Bhishma, who is famous for his will-power and abstinence.

Krishna was humble. Wondering how to utilise a non-combating Krishna, Arjuna requested him to be his charioteer. For a *Kshatriya*, that was a degrading occupation. When Shalya, the ruler of Madra was requested to be Karna's charioteer, he had got extremely annoyed. However, because Krishna was unassuming, he did not hesitate to take up the position of a charioteer.

To my mind, Sri Krishna's character was faultless and was full of virtues.

✦

Sanjaya's Mission

The two rival parties were preparing for the war. Even then, on Dhrupad's advice Yudhisthira sent Dhrupad's priest to Dhritarashtra's court urging for peace. The mission was in vain, of course, because Duryodhana was not ready to part with even as much land as the point of a needle could hold. However, Dhritarashtra, perceiving that in the event of a war, Bhima, Arjuna and Krishna would be immensely dangerous for the Kauravas, sent his secretary Sanjaya to advise Yudhisthira to desist from rivalry. This was absurd, indeed, for on the one hand, the Pandavas were not being given their due and on the other hand, they were asked not to fight for their right. The gist of Sanjaya's long speech to the Pandavas was that their entering a war would amount to *Adharma*.

So, addressing him, Yudhisthira said, "Oh Sanjaya, I do not desire for things that even gods wish for from the earth and I do not desire to acquire heavens by unethical means. But let Mahatma Krishna, who is a preacher of *Dharma*, who knows the laws, worships the *Brahmins*, has goodwill for the Pandavas and the Kauravas alike, point out what would be the valid course of action for me. For, I find that I stand to be blamed if I do not choose peace over war and I stand to be blamed if I do not fight for my right as a *Kshatriya*.... The influential Napta of Sini besides Chedi, Andhaka, Brishni, Bhoja, Kukura and Srinjaya sub-clans have defeated their enemies by following Krishna's intelligent advices. The brave and wise Yadavas, including Indra-like Ugrasena, are always advised by Krishna. With assistance and guidance from Krishna, Bavhru, the king of Kashi has acquired prosperity. Like the rains coming after summer,

Krishna showers him with desirables. Keshava has the qualities of a strategist; he is dear to us and he is goodness itself. I will never disregard what he says."

At this, Vasudeva said, "Oh Sanjaya, I constantly wish for the Pandavas' safety, prosperity and welfare and at the same time I wish Dhritarashtra's and his sons' rise of stature in society. I desire that the two parties reconcile and advise them to keep peace. When I am in the company of the Pandavas, I have often heard Yudhisthira wanting to have peace. However, Dhritarashtra and his sons are so greedy for wealth that any possibility of peace among the cousins seems remote. It would be hardly surprising, therefore, if friction intensifies. Oh Sanjaya, Yudhisthira and I have never wavered from the path of *Dharma*. Knowing this, why did you call Yudhisthira a non-follower of *Dharma*?"

Then Sri Krishna undertook to explain the nature of *Dharma*.

That Krishna undertook to explain the nature of *Dharma* points to an important feature of his character. We have mentioned that in his life Krishna tirelessly worked for two projects – the establishment of a righteous political system (i.e. the establishment of *Dharmarajya*), and the preaching of righteousness (*Dharma*).

The *Mahabharata* describes in detail Krishna's efforts of establishing a righteous political system. However, his preaching of righteousness is more or less limited in the *Gita*, which constitutes a part of *Bhishma Parva* of the *Mahabharata*.

Now, the question is how do we know that the *Gita* embodies Krishna's own unique idea of religion and not the idea of the poet who wrote it? Fortunately, we also find Krishna's preaching of this special religion in several other places of the *Mahabharata* besides the *Gita*. So, if we discover that what Krishna had preached elsewhere in the *Mahabharata* conforms with what he had preached in the *Gita*, then we can be sure that the religion of the *Gita* was conceived by Krishna himself.

Let us now examine what Krishna told Sanjaya that day, "Even though the scriptures maintain that one may lead a good life just by observing personal hygiene, by caring for one's people and by studying the *Vedas*, the *Brahmins* have their own ideas (about how to lead one's life). Some of them hold that only activities (i.e. rituals) can transport us to the Absolute, while others believe that only knowledge of the *Vedas*, detached from all practical work, takes us to the Absolute. Yet, just as hunger cannot be satiated without eating food, the Absolute cannot be met without doing any work except learning the *Vedas*. Such learning that teaches us to do something (worthwhile) is fruitful. Such learning that does not teach us to do something is useless. So, just as a thirsty person must drink water to quench his thirst, our duty in this world is to always strive for **practical solutions** to problems. Oh Sanjaya, this law is integral to the very nature of work (i.e. work is meant to solve problems). Therefore, (because of its problem-solving properties), work is superior to everything else in this world. Anyone who thinks otherwise (that work is not for solving problems) wastes his labour."

The doctrine of *Karma* (work) was practised even before it received Krishna's special attention. However, according to the earlier approach, *Karma* only meant the rituals described in the Vedas. The work that should be performed by a human being in his life, in the sense the term 'duty' is used in the West, was never meant by the word '*Karma*' in the religion prevalent in Krishna's time. In the *Gita*, the word differed from its earlier connotation and was prominently used in the sense of 'duty'. And, we find the word used in that particular sense in this part of the *Mahabharata* (i.e. in what Krishna says to Sanjaya). The language differs, but the narrator of the above quotation and the narrator of the *Gita* can be accepted as being one and the same.

To do well in what needs to be done, or to perform one's duty is one's *Dharma*. At the very beginning of the *Gita*, Sri Krishna advised Arjuna to do his duty. In the section of the *Mahabharata*, we are currently dealing with Krishna advised Sanjaya to do his duty by saying, "Oh Sanjaya, why did you, knowing well the respective duties of the *Brahmins*, the *Kshatriya*, the *Vaishyas* etc are trying for the fall of the Pandavas (i.e. obstructing them from performing their duty of regaining their rightful property as a *Kshatriya*) just for the benefit of the Kauravas? *Dharmaraja* Yudhisthira has Vedic knowledge, has performed the *Ashwamedha* and the *Rajasuya Yajna*, is well versed in the art of warfare and is a skilful elephant and horse rider. Now, instead of retaliating against the Kauravas, if the Pandavas, somehow calming down Bhima (as he is the most aggressive), can rescue their kingdom by some other means, they would be doing good work (of avoiding war and its pitfalls) and still be performing their duty. On the other hand, it would be fine even if they engage in a war and die fighting for their duty (of regaining their inherited kingdom). Probably you would prefer their agreeing to a compromise and giving up war. But I ask you, what would be dutiful for a *Kshatriya* – daring to be in a just war or abandoning it? Which, in your opinion, is superior? Tell me, and I would make my move according to that."

Sri Krishna then discoursed on the duties of the four different castes. What he said here is similar to what we find about that topic in the eighteenth chapter of the *Gita*. From other parts of the *Mahabharata* too, we find plenty of instances to show that the *Dharma* preached in the *Gita* is the same as that preached by Krishna elsewhere in the *Mahabharata*. This proves that the *Dharma* of the *Gita* was not merely named after Krishna but was actually conceived by him.

For the Europeans, there is nothing more desirable than capturing another's kingdom. They call it 'conquest', 'glory', 'extension of the empire', etc. Mesmerised by the idea of 'glorie', Fredrick II of Prussia consigned Europe to the flames of war thrice, causing destruction of lakhs of people. There is only one difference between such conquerors and the common thieves – conquerors steal large items while common thieves steal small things. Unfortunately, the allurement of world-conquest is so strong that even the Aryan *Kshatriyas* of India would lose their bearing sometimes and get infected by it. Diogenes had accused Alexander the Great by saying, "You are only a major bandit." In a similar vein, when any king got greedy in ancient India, Sri Krishna called him a prominent thief.

Like modern lawmakers, Krishna believed that it was honourable for one to protect one's property – that indeed it was one's sacred duty. In English language, resisting against a petty theft is called justice while resisting against a major aggression is called patriotism. The Indian word for both is *Dharma*. Krishna said, "Even at the cost of one's life one should not hesitate to recover one's inherited kingdom."

Irritated at Sanjaya's pretence of being a follower of *Dharma* and his misinterpretation of *Dharma* itself, Krishna rebuked him appropriately. He said, "You have now come to preach *Dharma* to Raja Yudhisthira but then (when Dushasana had harassed Draupadi in the courtroom) you did not preach *Dharma*." As a rule, Krishna spoke pleasantly to people. But, when he needed to criticise somebody, he did it in an unambiguous way, for he was always in favour of truth.

After chastising Sanjaya, Sri Krishna revealed that for the benefit of both the rival parties, he would himself go to Hastinapura on a mission of peace. He said, "We sincerely need to try finding some way by which the Pandavas can avoid financial loss while the Kauravas agree for peace – thereby saving themselves from destruction and death. Finding such a path would be a pious act indeed!"

For the common good, for the purpose of saving innumerable lives, for the well-being of even the Kauravas, Krishna himself took the initiative of working for this near-impossible objective. The project was all the more difficult for Krishna – and, after all, he was only a human being – because by then he had been officially chosen by the Pandavas to be on their side in the event of a war. This meant the Kauravas had gained the right to treat him as an enemy. Yet, for social good, Krishna decided to enter the enemy's court, unarmed.

◆

Proposal of Krishna's Visit to Hastinapura

Honouring his promise of approaching the Kauravas to try to work out a peaceful settlement, Sri Krishna prepared to leave for Hastinapura. The Pandavas as well as Draupadi had parting messages for him to all of which Sri Krishna replied patiently. Of course, those conversations cannot be taken as historical data but what the author of them made Krishna speak reveals that he was aware of who Krishna was and what he stood for. We would now quote extracts from those speeches.

On one occasion, in this context, Krishna answered to a question put to him by Yudhisthira by saying, "Oh Maharaja, the penance of *Brahmacharya* and other similar practices are not meant for the *Kshatriyas*. Begging (for example) for the *Kshatriyas* is largely forbidden by the hermits. God has divined victory or death in war to be a *Kshatriya's* duty, which he should constantly fulfil. Therefore, submissiveness is shameful for a *Kshatriya*. Oh Yudhisthira, overcome your apathy, you will never be able to regain your due if you are mild. Show valour and destroy your enemies."

In the *Gita*, too, we find Krishna speaking to Arjuna in a similar mode. I have already explained what conclusion we can draw from all this (i.e. that the religion offered in the *Gita* is Krishna's unique religion). Next, answering to a question put to him by Bhima, he said, "Man cannot lead his life just by depending on destiny or just by his own endeavour (i.e. destiny and hard work are equally important). One who believes this, is not sad when unsuccessful, or overly thrilled when successful."

The *Gita* also contains such statements. There, Krishna, answering to a question put to him by Arjuna spoke thus, "However fertile the land and however efficiently one ploughs and seeds it, getting a good yield of crop from it also depends on rain. The land may be destined for a drought even if someone tries his best to irrigate it. This is the reason why the great men of the past had decided that success can only come where fate and endeavour come together. I can engage myself in great humanly efforts, but I have no power over fate."

Thus once more Krishna totally denied possessing any divine power. He did this because, indeed, he was a human being dutifully acting out what he needed to do only with the strength of his humanly capabilities. If God intended to demonstrate his miraculous power, he would not require an agent, or messenger, to do that. Further, God's messenger, if he possessed divine power, would have no validity for ordinary men will not be able to follow him.

When the others had finished their say, Draupadi spoke to Krishna. What she said to him was quite unusual for a woman to utter. She said, "To not to kill someone who deserved to be slaughtered was as much a sin as killing a person who did not deserve that punishment."

Though it is surprising that the above statement had come from a lady, we cannot but accept that it is quite apt for the character of Draupadi that I sketched for *Bangadarshan* many years ago. And whether or not it sounds unpleasant when spoken by a lady, it does relate to what *Dharma* means and corresponds to Krishna's own belief. I have explained all this while writing about the slaying of Jarasandha.

The conclusion of Draupadi's speech, reproduced below, has superb poetry in it:

"Dark-complexioned Draupadi, agitated on hearing this, holding her elegant, snake-like tresses, addressed Krishna again, with tears and sadness in her eyes, Oh Janardana, wicked Dushasana had pulled these tresses. If the enemy proposes for peace, you remember these. Bhima and Arjuna like weaklings, have decided to make peace. That can hardly do me harm, though, as my elderly father, with his warrior sons, is going to fight my enemy. My five sons, brave and powerful, honouring Abhimanyu (by inviting him to join them), will destroy the Kauravas. How can I get peace of mind unless I find evil Dushasana's dirty arm, torn from his body, rolling in dust? My heart has been burning in anger for the past thirteen years. Now, even after thirteen years, I don't see any chance of its being satisfied. Today, hearing even Bhima speak of peace, my heart breaks!

Large-eyed, gorgeous Draupadi wept, her body trembling, her breasts drenching in hot tears. Dexterous Vasudeva, consoling her said, Oh Draupadi, within a few days you will find the Kaurava ladies in tears. They would be mourning their dead male relatives. Under the direction of Yudhisthira, Bhima, Arjuna, Nakula, Sahadeva and I will be able to destroy the Kauravas. If the sons of Dhritarashtra do not listen to me, they will fall and become the food of foxes and dogs. My prediction will hold true even if icy storm begins, and the earth shatters, and the sky falls with its celestial bodies. Oh Draupadi, control your tears. I tell you, within a few days you will certainly see your husbands winning back their kingdom after slaying their enemies."

The above speech is neither an emotional outburst of a dangerous, bloodthirsty being nor the heated words of an angry person. It is only the prediction about the future from a well-informed person with a very sharp intellect. Krishna knew for sure that Duryodhana would never agree to share his kingdom and bring about peace. That he was still prepared to approach the Kauravas with his proposal for peace was because of his belief that what needed to be done should be attempted even if it did not lead to success. He advocated that a person should have similar mental attitude towards success and failure. This is the focal point of Krishna's redeeming religion contained in the *Gita*. He taught Arjuna to make no difference between success and failure, but to work hard at what he had to do.

Following that notion, Krishna, the idealist, proceeded for the Kaurava court to campaign for peace even though he was sure of what the future held.

The Journey

Sri Krishna started his journey to Hastinapura in the manner of a gentleman of his time. He chose the *Maitra Muhurtama* of a day in the month of *Kartika* that was ruled by the *Revati Nakshatra*. To make the trip auspicious, he listened to benedictions of religious *Brahmins*, observed his morning cleansing, took his bath, dressed himself in clothes and jewellery, prayed to Fire and the Sun, viewed the bull and the plough along with other auspicious items, greeted the *Brahmins* and the Fire before taking his leave.

In his *Gita*, Sri Krishna has criticised the Brahminic rituals of the time – the rituals that were observed to fulfil personal desires. However, he never criticised the *Brahmins* themselves. As he was an ideally balanced person, he interacted with the *Brahmins* diplomatically and in the manner that was prevalent in his time. The *Brahmins* of that time were learned, knowledgeable, righteous and selfless, and they tried to serve the society. So, they rightly deserved respect from the other castes. This is the reason why Krishna also honoured them suitably. When on his way to Hastinapura, he met a group of *Brahmins*, he hurried to them and enquired about their whereabouts. It transpired that they too were heading for Hastinapura to listen to the discourses that were to be taking place in the Kaurava court. They said that they were especially looking forward to watch Krishna speak.

From the description of his journey to Hastinapura, we learn how Krishna was adored by the common people of his time:

"The son of Devaki (on his journey) viewed pretty and comfortable homes whose granaries were filled with all kinds of crop, pleasant village-animals, various localities and kingdoms. The contented, well-endowed, tranquil subjects of the Kuru clan had travelled from the town of Upaplavya to wait at roadsides to watch him as he passed.

When Mahatma Vasudeva arrived there, they worshipped him formally. Then, the sky turned russet as evening came. Madhusudhana, the dispeller of discord, reached a place where food was available. Dismounting his chariot immediately, he had a hygienic wash-up. Then, giving orders for the chariot horses to be set free, he started his evening prayers. Daruka, according to Krishna's wishes, unbridled the horses and competently massaged them to cure their stress.

Mahatma Madhusudhana, then, disclosed to his attendants that on his way to his mission for Yudhisthira, he would have to spend the night at the location they had arrived at. Hearing this, the attendants pitched up tents there and prepared delicious eatables and drinks. Thereafter, the members of the Brahmin community of that village, who were obedient followers of their *Dharma*, came to meet Mahatma Hrishikesha, the destroyer of disharmony. After worshipping and blessing him ritualistically, they invited him to their homes. Greeting them, Bhagwan Madhusudhana accepted their invitation.

Accompanying them to their dwellings, he invited them back to his own camp where they all partook of a delicious meal. Later Krishna spent the night in peace."

We find that the above description sketches the activities of a human being – a human being, however, who is extremely noble. There, nobody worships Krishna as a god. But he is worshipped like a great man and he himself behaves like a celebrity.

♦

Day One in Hastinapura

On hearing that Krishna was coming, aged Dhritarashtra got busy preparing to welcome him. He ordered that several halls be decorated with gems. He started collecting elephants, horses, servants, a hundred virgin maids, lambs, mules etc to gift Krishna.

Observing all this, Vidura said, "Oh well, I find that you are as clever as you are righteous! However, you can never win Krishna over with material things. Please him by agreeing to give what he is coming to ask for."

Dhritarashtra was cunning and Vidura was naïve. Duryodhana was both. He said, "Even though Krishna deserves to be honoured, we would not honour him. As we would never agree to his suggestion that we need desist from aggression, where is the necessity of treating him well? People will think that we are trying to placate Krishna out of fear. I have a better strategy. Let us catch and tether him. Krishna is the Pandavas' strength and intellectual asset. If he is detained, the Pandavas would remain under my power."

These words made even Dhritarashtra angry with his eldest son, because Krishna was coming to them as an emissary (with faith in the Kauravas' good manners). And Bhishma, the devotee of Krishna, was so irritated that he left the assembly after hurling harsh words at Duryodhana.

Soon, the citizens of Hastinapura and several members of the Kaurava family brought Krishna into the court with high honour.

Barely glancing at the beautiful halls prepared for him and ignoring the gifts kept for him, Krishna came directly where Dhritarashtra was seated. Taking a seat, he addressed each member of the group according to his status. Later, Krishna, the friend of the poor, left the palace and walked towards the home of a person of humble means.

The person he went to meet was Vidura, the step-brother of Dhritarashtra. Both Dhritarashtra and Vidura were the biological sons of Veda Vyasa. However, while Dhritarashtra's mother was the legally wedded wife of King Vichitravirya, Vidura's mother was a *Vaishya* maid servant of Vichitravirya. (As such, according to the custom of that time, Dhritarashtra was considered to be a true son of Vichitravirya, while Vidura was not considered as his son at all).

A simple person, Vidura was a great follower of *Dharma*. Leaving the Kaurava palace, Krishna came to Vidura's abode and accepted his hospitality. Kunti, the mother of the Pandavas and Krishna's paternal aunt, was staying there. The Pandavas had left her with Vidura before they left for the forests.

When Krishna went to Kunti to pay her his respects, Kunti wept a lot remembering that her sons and her daughter-in-law were spending a rigorous time in the jungles. Krishna's remark in reply is worthy of notice. He said, "The Pandava brothers, by conquering sleep, lethargy, hunger, thirst, cold, heat and merriment are relishing the joy of being brave. Sacrificing the pleasures of the senses, they are immersed in the ecstasy of daring. Those mighty dauntless ones, full of enthusiasm, are never easily satisfied. Gallant men like them experience either acute pain or intense happiness. On the other hand, mediocre men, involved in the pleasures of the senses, who do not endeavour for the highest goals, remain unhappy. Conquering one's kingdom or living in the forests (i.e. achieving one's goal or doing whatever is necessary to achieve it) are both – bliss."

Unfortunately, most Hindus do not understand what Krishna meant by, "Conquering one's kingdom or living in the forests." If they did they would not have suffered so much.

Krishna also assured Kunti that she would soon find her sons victorious and prosperous.

This meant that Krishna was conscious that appeasement would not come about, that war was inevitable. Yet he had come to Hastinapura to negotiate for a reconciliation only because what needed to be done had to be attempted. One had to do one's duty irrespective of what came in return. This is what Krishna describes in his *Gita* as Karma Yoga. As a peaceful settlement between the two parties had to be attempted because that was a better option than war for the community they both belonged to. Yet when reconciliation failed in spite of his most sincere efforts and confrontation became a necessity, Krishna himself became the disillusioned Arjun's motivator and guide. This was because reconciliation being ruled out confrontation remained as the only option and so became an indispensable duty. Thus, we find that Krishna himself was the principle follower of the religion he preached in his *Gita*.

Krishna spent the night in Vidura's house engaged in discussions with him. Vidura opined that Krishna's coming to Hastinapura was a mistake as Duryodhana would never agree to a compromise. To quote from Krishna's reply, "The person who does not try to save his friend from folly is labelled as inhuman by the wise men. The knowledgeable would prevent his friend from doing wrong even by pulling his hair. I do not have any trouble if Duryodhana loses faith in me after hearing my sagacious words. I can at least draw satisfaction from the fact that I had given my kin good advice. The person who does not try to prevent division among his near ones is unworthy of being called a relative."

◆

Day Two in Hastinapura

Next morning Duryodhana and Shakuni arrived early in Vidura's house to escort Krishna to the Kaurava court. There, a great conference was held. Divinities like Narada *Rishi* and great ascetics like Jamadagni *Rishi* arrived to attend the meeting. In a long, well-delivered speech, Krishna tried to persuade Dhritarashtra to accept a proposal of reconciliation. The *rishis* supported him. However, Dhritarashtra remained unmoved. His response was, "I am helpless in this matter. Talk to Duryodhana."

Krishna, Bhishma, Drona and others took their turns in reasoning with Duryodhana, but they only made him angry. And he ended up by insulting Krishna with harsh words. Krishna replied harshly, too. When he accused Duryodhana of bad character and sinfulness, Duryodhana left the meeting in disgust.

Next, Krishna advised Dhritarashtra to act according to the principles of statesmanship which held that a sovereign, to protect his subjects, had to punish criminals. It was advisable to punish a few for the benefit of many. The wise held that the culprit who could cause the death of thousands if left free should be imprisoned. This was the reason why European rulers and their ministers had imprisoned Napoleon for life in 1815. On the same principle, Krishna advised Dhritarashtra to imprison Duryodhana and make peace with the Pandavas. He himself, he reminded his host, had killed his own uncle Kansa to save the Yadava clan.

It goes without saying that Krishna's advice fell on deaf ears.

In the meantime, the angry Duryodhana began to conspire with Karna a move to capture Krishna. Krishna's relatives Satyaki, Kritavarma and others were present at the court. Satyaki was a devoted follower of Krishna. A student of Arjuna in the art of weaponry, he was almost as competent a warrior as his master. Extremely sharp of intellect, he was an expert in deciphering body language. Satyaki guessed what Karna and Duryodhana had in mind. Advising Kritavarma and another Yadava stalwarts to take position at the entrance of the meeting hall with armed men, he alerted Krishna about the danger. He also revealed the plot of capturing Krishna to the entire court. At this, Vidura reacted by addressing Dhritarashtra and asking him, "Aren't these people acting like insects who throw themselves into fire? For, if Janardana wishes to retaliate, he can destroy all of them when war breaks out."

When Krishna addressed Dhritarashtra, though, he was respectful to him. Sure of his own strength, he was forgiving and amiable. He said, "I hear that Duryodhana and his men have become so angry with me that they want to forcefully capture me. But with your permission, I can single-handedly arrest them all. However, I would never do something which is so base and sinful. On the other hand, greed for the Pandavas' wealth would misguide your sons. In fact, by wanting to detain me, they are assisting Yudhisthira. For, I can capture all of them today and present them to Yudhisthira and because of their attitude towards us nobody would blame me for doing that. However, in your presence, I would hate to take up such spiteful actions. Let Duryodhana command his followers to execute his evil biddings."

Dhritarashtra, at this, summoned Duryodhana near him and rebuked him for assuming that he could capture Krishna whom even gods were unable to defeat. Vidura, too, admonished Duryodhana. Laughing loudly at his antagonist's humiliation, Vasudeva, then, left the court holding the hands of his friends Satyaki and Kritavarma.

Till this point of its narrative, the *Mahabharata* describes Krishna's mission of peace in a logical and natural way. There is no confusion anywhere, no unbelievable or supernatural incidences. However, the impatient interpolators of the narrative could not tolerate this. How could they prove that Krishna was a god without linking such an important episode to some supernatural occurrence? Probably that question in their minds had led the interpolators to insert the story of

Krishna revealing the Cosmos – the *vishwarupa* – in himself, after he laughed and before he left the court. In the *Mahabharata, Bhishma Parva* which contains the *Bhagavata Gita*, we find Krishna's similar *vishwarupa darshan* or the revelation of the Universe in himself. The description of that revelation, granting that that version too might be interpolated, is much superior to the revelation mentioned during Krishna's peace mission. The former is the work of a first rate poet and is a fine specimen of world class literature, the latter is hardly poetic.

Even idiots do not act needlessly, not to speak of someone who is supposed to embody the Universe itself. In the latter case, there is not the slightest need for Krishna to reveal the Cosmos in himself. Duryodhana and his party were only considering whether to use force. They did not actually try to use force. Admonished by father and uncle, Duryodhana had remained silent. Moreover, Krishna was confident that any attempt to use force to capture him would be futile. For, even if his own power was not enough for his self-defence, the mighty warriors of the Vrishna sub-clan like Kritavarma and Satyaki were present there to assist him. Certainly, therefore, there was no reason, at that point, for Krishna to manifest himself in a cosmic role even if he were God.

So, it is advisable to reject this incident of celestial revelation as the miscreation of an inferior poet. I have repeatedly shown that Krishna acted only with his humanly power and not with any divine superpower. There is no reason to believe that there was an exception at this episode.

From the Kuru court, Krishna went to meet Kunti. From there, he proceeded to the city of Upaplavya, where the Pandavas were staying. Before leaving, he had Karna join him on his *Ratha*.

Karna was a member of the group that had considered arresting Krishna. In the next chapter, I will recount why Krishna still gave Karna a ride on his own vehicle. That account will vividly illustrate Krishna's character. We have seen Krishna's proficiency in diplomacy and law-enforcement. Now we will see his competence in utilising differences. Together with that we will find how Krishna was really an ideal person with his compassion, goodwill and intellect superior to all.

Krishna's Meeting with Karna

Krishna was merciful to all. He was the only *Kshatriya* who was saddened by the thought of the huge loss of life the impending war was threatening to bring. When in Virata's city, the proposal of a war first came up, Krishna had counselled against it. When Arjuna came to embrace him to fight on his side, he offered himself to him only as a non-combatant supporter. However, in spite of his efforts, the war was about to begin. Having no alternative, he, therefore, went to Dhritarashtra's court himself to plead for reconciliation, convinced though he was of the futility of his mission. His efforts failed, as expected. Tragic slaughter of men became inevitable. So Krishna, the statesman contrived to find other ways of stopping the war.

Karna was a hero. As a warrior, he matched Arjuna. Karna's strength was one reason why Duryodhana felt powerful. Duryodhana's belief in Karna's strength was the primary factor responsible for his choosing to fight the Pandavas. Without Karna's assistance, he would never fight. If ever Duryodhana discovered Karna assisting the enemy, he would desist from war. To bring about such a state of affair, Krishna took Karna on his chariot. It was necessary to speak to him in private.

Convincing Karna to join the Pandavas seemed easy for Krishna. For, unknown to others, he knew some important secret about that warrior's past.

Karna was known to be the son of Adhiratha, the *Suta*. But, in fact, he was Adhiratha's adopted son. Karna himself was unaware of this truth. Conceiving Karna through Surya, Kunti was his mother. Because he was a child born out of wedlock, Kunti had abandoned him soon after his birth. Thus, being born of the same mother, Karna was actually the eldest brother of the Pandavas. Krishna knew about this fact of Karna's origin. To his sharp intellect, things got easily revealed. Moreover, Kunti was his aunt on his father's side and Karna's birth had taken place in the household of Bhoja Raja, Krishna's relative. So it was quite possible that Krishna, an intelligent perceiver, would have garnered the information.

Aboard the chariot, Krishna related the particulars of his birth to Karna. He added, "Scholars who are familiar with the scriptures say that by marrying a girl, the husband automatically becomes the father of any child she might be already carrying and any child she might have had out of wedlock. You too were born before your mother was married. So you are rightfully a son of your mother's husband. You shall become a king." He explained to Karna that as the eldest brother he would be the ruler while the five other Pandavas would follow his commands and attend to his needs.

This recommendation of Krishna was for everybody's benefit and was based on *Dharma*. It was good for Karna too, as not only would he become a ruler but also reconciled with his own brothers. This could save Duryodhana from destruction, as in the event of an war, it was almost certain that he would lose all his kinsmen as well as his kingdom. If war could be avoided, Duryodhana would live and enjoy his kingdom. He would only have to part with what rightfully belonged to the Pandavas. This would be beneficial and morally desirable for the Pandavas as well, as they would be able to enjoy their land along with Karna without having to engage in a cruel war, which was sure to massacre many of their relatives. Above all, the merit of this proposition was that it could save innumerable human lives.

Karna, too, acknowledged the advantages of Krishna's proposal. He, too, had realised that Duryodhana and his evil faction had no chance of surviving the war. But, to follow Krishna advice, he himself would have to commit grave offences. Adhiratha and Radha had brought him up. Living under their protection, he had married into the *Suta* clan and had begotten children and grandchildren with his *Suta* wife. On no account would he abandon them. Moreover, under the care of Duryodhana, he had enjoyed a kingdom for thirteen years. Duryodhana trusted him. If he left Duryodhana now and joined the Pandavas, people would call him ungrateful, greedy for the Pandavas' wealth or a coward terrified of their strength. For all those reasons, Karna was adamant not to comply with Krishna's proposal.

Krishna said, "Now that my words could not move you, I am sure that the world is coming to its doom."

After some appropriate reply, Karna hugged Krishna and left him with a heavy heart.

We do not need to discuss Karna in detail to understand the character of Krishna. So I have not taken it up here. Karna as a person was exceedingly noble and pleasing.

◆

Section - VI
Kurukshetra

Bhishma in Battle

The time eventually came for the war of Kurukshetra to take place. The *Mahabharata* describes it in four chapters. The chapters are named after four successive generals of Duryodhana as *Bhishma Parva*, *Drona Parva*, *Karna Parva* and *Shalya Parva*.

The chapters concerning the war should be considered as belonging to the shabbily written part of the *Mahabharata*. Repetition, unnecessary or uncouth excesses of description, unnatural occurrences, exaggeration and inconsistencies are the faults of this section. Very little of the stark, original *Mahabharata* seems to belong here. Yet, even here, it is very difficult to separate the original parts from the unoriginal parts. It is as difficult as plucking flowers from a thorn bush. In spite of this difficulty, we would pay special attention even here to any data that refers to Krishna's character.

In the *Bhishma Parva*, after some casual mention of Krishna, comes the *Gita*. The *Gita* is the primary material that throws light on Krishna's character. Spreading the religion of the *Gita* was Krishna's goal in life. And, the *Gita* reveals the identity of Krishna better than any other source.

However, I will not mention anything about the *Gita* here, as I have already discussed it in my *Dharmatatva* and am engaged in writing a commentary on the *Gita* itself.

In the *Mahabharata*, after the chapter on *Bhagavata Gita*, comes the chapter of Bhishma's fall. The actual war of Kurukshetra begins with that incident. In the war, Krishna is merely Arjuna's charioteer.

Charioteers at that time were considered ill-fated people. As described in the *Mahabharata*, a war fought at that time consisted only of a series of one to one chariot encounters. Warriors on their chariots would try to destroy other chariots and horses to put their foes in peril. The charioteers, who were not warriors would be killed without giving any tangible contribution to the actual fight. Krishna, too, had to put himself in such an unattractive position.

Even though he was not killed in the eighteen days' war, he was wounded every day by innumerable arrows. The other charioteers were incapable of self-defence as they were *Vaishyas* and so untrained in the technique of warfare. Krishna, on the other hand, was amply capable of self-defence, and yet, duty-bound, he bore all the 'slings and arrows of outrageous fortune' without resistance.

Krishna had resolved not to take up arms in the war of the *Mahabharata*. However, he did take it up one day. He did not use it, though, ultimately. The incident happened as follows:

Bhishma, in his capacity of Duryodhana's general, was such an expert in the use of arms that no one in the Pandava army, except Arjuna, could equal him. Yet Arjuna was not using his ability to the full when he encountered Bhishma. This was happening because Bhishma was Arjuna's grandfather and had brought him and the other fatherless Pandavas up like his own sons. At Duryodhana's urging, Bhishma was fighting the Pandavas as if they were his enemies. This gave Arjuna the right to kill him. But overcome with memories of the past, he was unable to do so. He was attacking Bhishma only mildly, ever careful not to kill him. Taking advantage of Arjuna's weakness, on the other hand, Bhishma, with unchallenged bravery, was slaying numerous Pandava soldiers. Observing this day after day, Krishna, on one occasion, climbed down from Arjuna's *Ratha*, with discus in his hand and ran on foot as if intending to kill Bhishma himself.

Bhishma, the Krishna-worshipper, was delighted at this, and invited him, with intense devotion, to fell him (Bhishma) from his great chariot.

Arjuna followed Krishna, pleading him to return, promising to fight to the best of his own ability from then on. Somehow, he brought Krishna back.

The above incident has been described twice in the *Mahabharata* – once on day three of the war and once on day nine. And, the same verse is used in both the cases indicating that the copier, mistakenly or by choice, wrote it twice. Such repetitions are quite common in Sanskrit books.

Judging by its style, the account in context seems to belong to the genuine layer of the *Mahabharata*. The poetry expressed here is first rate, with thought and language noble and uncomplicated. The tone of authenticity that this part bears is shared by the core area of the *Mahabharata*. Krishna-worshippers have found strange explanations about this particular incident. They say that Bhishma at the beginning of the war had promised to break Krishna's vow of not taking up arms. So, Krishna, out of love for his devotee, had broken his own vow.

However, we find no reason to accept the above explanation. And in the original *Mahabharata*, we do not find this story of Bhishma's resolve of breaking Krishna's vow. Moreover, Krishna had, in fact, not broken his vow. For the essence of his vow was that he would not fight. To be impartial to both Duryodhana and Arjuna, he had offered himself to one side as a non-combating participant in lieu of his *Narayani* soldiers for the other side. Krishna had kept that promise by not fighting. Chasing Bhishma with discus in hand was only to provoke Arjuna to fight better. Charioteers used to take such steps. And in this case, the mission had been accomplished.

After nine days' war, Krishna, for the same reason, had said that he wanted to kill Bhishma. Finding Bhishma invincible, Yudhisthira was holding a meeting with his friends at night to devise a way of killing him. Krishna offered to kill Bhishma himself if given the permission. Otherwise, he said, Arjuna could kill him as he definitely had that ability.

Yudhisthira did not agree to Krishna killing Bhishma. He said, "I do not want to make you a liar just for enhancing my own prestige. Assist us only as a non-fighter." Later, it is said, they went to Bhishma who himself told them how he should be killed. And apparently, he was killed when the Pandavas followed that instruction. However, what really happened was that Arjuna felled him in a straight fight – just what Krishna was expecting him to do. Some poet belonging to what we call the second layer of the *Mahabharata* had made up an attractive but unnecessary and inconsistent story.

Jayadratha Killed

After Bhishma's fall, Dronocharya became Duryodhana's general. In the beginning of *Drona Parva*, Krishna is not involved in any special way in the war other than efficiently manoeuvring Arjuna's chariot just like an expert charioteer should do. Judging from this part of the *Mahabharata*, it will not be true to say that the war of Kurukshetra was brought about by Krishna and was executed under his leadership. He does not do much here except delivering good advices to Arjuna and Yudhisthira from time to time. In chapter eleven of *Dronabhisheka* (appointment of Drona), there is an unnecessarily lengthy description of Krishna's might and bravery by Sanjaya. This portion seems to be interpolated. Indeed, in the *Mahabharata* and elsewhere, there is no dearth of verses reciting Krishna's glory. However, here we are engaged in analysing his human qualities and those qualities can only be manifested through the work he did.

In *Drona Parva*, we find Krishna's first active involvement in the killing of Bhagadatta. Bhagadatta was such a mighty hero that very few in the Pandavas' side could fight with him. After many of them failed to contain him, Arjuna himself took up the task. Finding himself too weak against Arjuna, Bhagadatta aimed the *Vaishnavastra* at him. Nobody, not even Arjuna, could stop that weapon. So Krishna screened Arjuna with his own body and took the weapon on his own chest. The weapon transforming into a wreath of *Vaijayanty* flowers ended up by adorning Krishna's neck.

The above story about the *Vaishnavastra* is supernatural and incomprehensible. We do not ask our readers to believe in what is supernatural and we do not base any of our findings on them. We reject the story summarily.

In *Drona Parva*, we find Krishna actually taking up action on the field only after Abhimanyu was killed. On that day seven, warriors surrounded Abhimanyu and killed him unfairly. Krishna and Arjuna were not present at that part of the battlefield. Both of them were engaged elsewhere in fighting the *Narayani* soldiers – the battalion Krishna had given to Duryodhana.

Returning to camp after the end of the day's war, they heard how Abhimanyu was killed. Arjuna was deeply grieved. However, Krishna, master of self-control, was above grief and attachment. His priority was to calm Arjuna. The words he used to console him could belong only to Krishna. Those words conform with the religion he had preached in the *Gita*. The *Rishis* were consoling Yudhisthira by saying that everybody must die. Krishna, however, did not say that. He explained, "*Kshatriyas* are professional warriors. It is but natural, therefore, that they would die in battle."

Krishna consoled Abhimanyu's mother Subhadra with similar words. He said, "You son died in the manner in which a steady and high-born *Kshatriya* should die. His death need not be mourned. Heroic and steadfast, Abhimanyu, as valiant as his father, was lucky to achieve the end that the brave wish for. The supremely courageous Abhimanyu, after destroying numerous opponents has left for the eternal abode of the meritorious where everything that can be desired is met. The end the holy men seek by penance, celibacy, learning from the scriptures and thinking has been awarded to your son. Oh Subhadra, you are the mother of a brave son, the wife of a brave husband, the daughter of a brave father and the sister of brave brothers. It is not for you to get carried away by the sorrow of your son's death."

I know that a mother cannot forget her sorrow by hearing all that. But I would want my unfortunate countrymen to listen to such words and to speak such words.

Meanwhile, grief-stricken by his son's death, Arjuna rashly burdened himself with a terrible oath. From what he heard of the incident, he concluded that Jayadratha was the main cause of Abhimanyu's death. He took the vow that he would kill Jayadratha before sunset the next day or burn himself to death.

The news of that oath agitated both the camps. The Pandava band began to play loudly. The Kauravas began to discuss ways of protecting Jayadratha.

Krishna realised the danger of the situation. It would be difficult to keep the vow that Arjuna had foolhardily made. Jayadratha, a great warrior and the ruler of Sindhusoubir, himself had a large army. And he was Duryodhana's brother-in-law. The invincible soldiers of the Kaurava camp would try to protect him to their utmost. On the other hand, the leading figures of the Pandava camp, overwhelmed by Abhimanyu's demise, had no interest even in any kind of discussions. So, Krishna, taking charge of the situation, sent his spy to the enemy camp. The spy brought back the news that Duryodhana was about to form a difficult unit of warriors with Karna and other Kaurava greats, to jointly protect Jayadratha. It might not be possible even for Arjuna to penetrate that awesome formation, defeat all the warriors in it, and kill Jayadratha.

So Krishna, electing to do something himself, readied himself to take action. He summoned his own charioteer Daruka and instructed him to keep his chariot ready at dawn with good horses and lots of weapons. He intended to fight himself to help Arjuna in case Arjuna did not reach Jayadratha within the formation of heroes, in a day's time.

As it happened, Krishna did not need to fight. Arjuna succeeded in reaching his goal by his own strength. However, even if Krishna had fought in this case, he would not have broken his vow of remaining a non-combatant in the war because this was a different kind of conflict altogether. It was not the war over a kingdom which the Kurus and the Pandavas were fighting. The confrontation that originated out of Arjuna's vow to kill Jayadratha had a different aim. The clash was over Jayadratha's and Arjuna's lives. If Arjuna lost, he would have to burn himself to death. This particular clash did not exist earlier when Krishna had vowed not to take up arms in the war of the Kurus and the Pandavas. So Krishna's vow of not taking up weapons did not extend to this particular battle. Arjuna was Krishna's friend, pupil and brother-in-law. It was his duty to prevent Arjuna from committing suicide.

✦

Understanding the Work of the Later Poets

So far our subject of study was like a calm sea. Now, it would become turbulent. This is because we have now fallen into the hands of a different brand of poet who elaborately builds upon the core story of the *Mahabharata*. This poet changed the character of Krishna completely. Where there was large-heartedness, he brought in pettiness and meanness, what was simple became pretentious, what was straightforward became full of untruth and deception. In place of justice and *Dharma*, injustice and *Adharma* came. In the hands of this second category poet, Krishna developed many faults in his character.

But why did this happen? This type two poet is not too bad as a poet, as such. His poetic ability does shine through. And we find that he was not ignorant of *Dharma*. Then why did he put Krishna in such a pathetic condition? Actually, there is a vitally important reason for what he did.

Firstly, we have seen and shall see again and again how Krishna is not presented as divine incarnation by the poet of the core *Mahabharata*. In the earlier poet's work, Krishna does not even once mention that himself. Over and over again, he expresses himself and identifies himself as a human being. And he does his work with human abilities. So we can suspect that when this layer of the *Mahabharata* was composed, Krishna was not commonly acknowledged as a divine incarnation. Basically, the first layer of the *Mahabharata* is just a compilation of ancient legends strung together in verse. However, by the time the second layer of writing was added and absorbed into the story of the *Mahabharata*, Krishna's divinity was probably universally recognised.

Therefore, the poet of this layer of the *Mahabharata* established Krishna as if he were an *avatar* – incarnation of God.

In this poet's composition, even Krishna himself identifies himself as divine on several occasions and applies superhuman power to carry out his work.

The later poet of the *Mahabharata* does not stop there. He goes on to explore the nature of God and particularly engages himself in explaining the complex philosophical concern: If God is all-powerful, why does He not remove sorrow from earth? The European people, too, are deeply puzzled by this question. The problem confuses them thoroughly because they are convinced that God is compassionate and has created living beings out of His own compassion. And God, they believe, always wishes His creatures well. Then, why is there evil on earth?

The question does not baffle the Hindus as much as it does the Europeans. This is because the Hindus believe that God encompasses the entire Universe which includes both good and evil. And the poet of the second stratum of the *Mahabharata* is anxious to illustrate this vital ideology. According to the Hindus, the world is God's creation and a mere plaything for Him. In that world, virtue and vice co-exist. But God does not differentiate between them. He is impartial as He is the essence of everything. Nothing, not even evil, can exist without God. The difference between good and evil in the world is but our illusion.

Because virtue and vice both originate from God, the poet of the *Vishnu Purana* makes Kalia, the serpent who was tortured by Krishna say, "You yourself have created me as a snake and therefore I am ruthless."

Similarly, Prahlad prays to Vishnu by saying, "Thou art knowledge and ignorance, truth and untruth, poison and nectar."

In the *Gita*, Krishna himself says, "The dispositions of virtue, authoritativeness, and malice are all mine. But I am not controlled by them. They are under my control." In the *Shanti Parva* of the *Mahabharata* where Bhishma praises Krishna as, "My obeisance to the one who is eternally pure. My obeisance to the one who is righteousness personified." He also praises him as 'one who has unlimited craving' and 'one who is dreadful and apparently cruel'. Hundreds of pages can be filled by similar quotations from ancient scriptures of the Hindus. And this aspect of Hinduism is infused into the verses of the type two poet of the *Mahabharata*.

The great poets of the ancient world did not explain their messages in the introductions of their works like the authors of today. We have to carefully identify the essence of their expressions from their actual compositions. To understand and communicate the underlying meaning of each of Shakespeare's plays, thousands of bright scholars have thought deeply and written voluminously. And we (the Indians) have taken great pains to go through those writings in order to appreciate the mysteries of Shakespeare's creations. Yet we have never made even an hour's effort to realise the underlying meaning of even a single chapter of the unique treatise that is our *Mahabharata*. The saddest part is that even when someone has wanted to explain it to us we have not bothered to pay attention.

God is omnipresent. Everything is contained in Him. He is knowledge and ignorance, wisdom and folly, truth and untruth, justice and injustice. However, while it is easy for a human being to comprehend that knowledge, intelligence, truth and justice stem from Him, it is not easy for ordinary mortals to accept that God is also the source of negative concepts, like error and ignorance. Yet, it is necessary for man to understand that. At least that is the opinion of the poet of the second stratum of the *Mahabharata*. Modern astronomers say that we can see just one side of the moon. The other side always remains invisible for us. The brand two poet of the second layer of the *Mahabharata* wished to give us a glimpse of the reverse side of our idea of God (like an astronomer trying to show us how the other side of the moon looks). In the killing of Jayadratha, the poet shows us that error comes from God; through Ghatotkacha's death he tells that folly, too, comes from God, by the slaying of Drona, he counts untruth as an aspect of God and through the killing of Duryodhana, he reveals that even injustice is part of Him.

◆

The Fall of Ghatotkacha

The poet who describes the episode of Ghatotkacha's fall depicts Krishna in a very undignified light:

A *Rakshasa* called Hidimbo had a sister called Hidimba. Once upon a time, Bhima killed Hidimbo and married Hidimba. (If you ask me, I think it was a perfect match!) They had a son called Ghatotkacha, who too turned out to be a *Rakshasa*. He grew up to become a strong, young giant. In the Kurukshetra war, he was fighting with his army to help his father and uncles. Unfortunately for him, a *Rakshasa* was fighting for Duryodhana also. The two zealous giants clashed fiercely.

On one occasion, the war was going through an especially fearsome patch. The various confrontations continued late into the night with the help of myriad torches. Nocturnal creatures develop additional strength at night. *Rakshasas* being nocturnal creatures Ghatotkacha seemed insurmountable. The Kaurava heroes were scared to confront him and the Kaurava giant had been slain. Karna, alone, had the courage to challenge Ghatotkacha and his troop. But he too was losing. In desperation, the hero (Karna) took out his most valuable weapon, which he had kept in reserve for Arjuna's destruction. This weapon which was gifted to him by Indra was called *Ekapurushaghatani*, that is, the killer of one person. When targeted at someone, this weapon was sure to kill him. However, after that, the weapon would be gone forever. Striking Ghatotkacha with *Ekapurushaghatani*, Karna killed him. At the time of his death, Ghatotkacha enlarged his body so much that it covered the foothills of mountain Vindhyachala crushing one *aksauhinis* enemy soldiers.

Such exaggeration and excesses of sensationalism by an ancient Hindu poet should be pardoned – tactics such as these had to be used to thrill illiterate women and children. However what the poet composed next is so uncouth that I wonder if it was meant to entertain nobody but himself! The poet states that while the Pandava brothers were mourning the demise of Ghatotkacha, Krishna was ecstatically dancing in joy abode his chariot. This image of Krishna is totally opposed to his public image found so far in the *Mahabharata* where, in his social life, he always appeared to be dignified and composed.

When Arjuna asked him the reason for his cheer, Krishna replied that he was celebrating the fact that *Ekapurushaghatani* was spent on Ghatotkacha sparing Arjuna's life. "You will now be able to attack Karna without fear," Krishna added. Oddly, when Karna and Arjuna had repeatedly fought each other in the wake of Jayadratha's death, nobody, not even the poet himself, remembered Indra's weapon! Clearly, the weapon, if used at that stage, would hinder Jayadratha's killing and interfere with the plot of the main story. This proves that the weapon in context was totally fabulous.

After Ghatotkacha's death, Krishna said to Arjuna, "Dear Dhananjaya, for your welfare, by using various strategies, I have brought about the death of Jarasandha, Shishupala, the Nishada Ekalavya, Hidimbo, Kirmira, Baka, Alayudha, Ugrakarma and other *Rakshasas*."

The above statement is factually incorrect. For, most of the projects mentioned in it did not directly benefit Arjuna. Moreover, Krishna was not connected, in any way, in the killings of the *Rakshasas* Baka, Hidimbo, or Kirmira.

What is the reason for the poet of this statement to make Krishna tell such obvious lies except to mean that even God can speak lies, or in other words, that even untruth dwells in God?

Some devotees of Krishna may say that Krishna had achieved all that he claimed in the above statement in the sense that he had willed them to happen. But then, Krishna had referred to having used 'various strategies', which is different from just 'willing'.

The actual message of Krishna's statement is what I have elaborated in my previous chapter. The poet wants to say that knowledge, stupidity and ignorance all come from God. Karna used Indra's weapon on

Ghatotkacha instead of Arjuna. This was Karna's folly. The poet wants to say that it was one of Krishna's 'strategies', that is, it was Krishna, the God, who had put folly in Karna's mind. It was God-sent folly in Shishupala's mind, again, that made him taunt Krishna in a crowded *Sabha*. Jarasandha, with a large army under his command, was powerful enough to defeat the Yadavas. However, as an individual wrestler, Bhima was stronger than him. It was Jarasandha's folly that he chose to fight a duel with Bhima. This folly, according to the poet, was God-sent. It was non-Aryan Ekalavya's folly that he sacrificed his right thumb – ruining his career as an archer – to please a cruel *Brahmin*. Ekalavya's error of judgement, according to Krishna's statement given earlier, was also sent by God.

To sum up, the verses of the *Mahabharata* relating to the fall of Ghatotkacha belong to the second stratum of the epic with a perspective much different from the core segment of the *Mahabharata*.[5]

◆

---

[5] *Translator's Footnote*
Moreover, the fact that the poet of 'The Fall of Ghatotkacha' – a story concocted for mass appeal – so freely deals with *Advaitavada* (the belief in an all-inclusive reality), indicates that this tract was composed at a comparatively later period. For, in the early days of the *Vedas* and the *Upanishads*, philosophic learning was esoteric, that is, taught only to select pupils seated close to (*upasana*) the teacher. It was Adi Shankaracharya, born around the year 686 AD, who for the first time in India, exposed the common man to the content of the *Vedas*.

The Fall of Drona

In ancient India, the *Kshatriyas* were the warrior class. However, that did not mean that the other classes never participated in a war. In the *Mahabharata* itself, we find references to *Brahmin* and *Vaishya* men fighting. Among the generals of Duryodhana, the three most important ones were *Brahmins* – Drona, his son Asvatthama, and his brother-in-law Kripa. *Brahmins*, in those days, were the teachers of all the branches of studies including the techniques of warfare. This is the reason why Drona and his brother-in-law, Kripa, were known as Dronacharya (Master Drona) and Kripacharya (Master Kripa) respectively.

Now, according to the social code of the time, killing a *Brahmin*, even in a war, was a sin. This rule created a problem for the authors of the *Mahabharata* when they had to deal with any *Brahmin* casualty of war. How, for example, could they say that their heroes, the Pandavas, or any of their friends, had killed a *Brahmin*? To bypass this problem, they kept Kripacharya and Asvatthama alive even after the war. The Kurukshetra war had left everyone on the Kaurava side dead except the two Brahmins just named. However, the problem with Dronacharya was more complex. He had taken charge of the Kaurava army immediately after Bhishma's fall. His death was essential for the Pandavas' victory. And yet, even Arjuna, the most capable archer of the Pandava camp, was forbidden to kill him, not only because Drona was a *Brahmin*, but also because he was Arjuna's guru or revered teacher.

So the author of this tract of the *Mahabharata* was forced to contrive a way out. He did this by fabricating a story. According to that story, Drona had once disgraced Draupadi's father King Dhrupad. This had led Dhrupad to perform a *Yajna* that would give him the power of killing Drona and had received a son, called Dhristadyumna, from the sacrificial pit. Thus, Dhristadyumna was specially born to grow up as Drona's nemesis.

In the Kurukshetra war, we find Dhristadyumna acting as the commander of the Pandava army. The Pandavas entrusted him with the task of felling Drona, for as a being created by a sacred ritual just for that purpose, the sin of Brahminicide would not touch him. The ground was thus prepared for Drona's fall without damaging the Pandavas' image.

However, the *Mahabharata* is not the work of a single poet. Many different composers have contributed to it. And the storyline had to change according to their individual fancies. So Drona did not die immediately. Another poet had taken over the plot. As he relates, Dhristadyumna could not harm Drona even after fifteen days' intense battle. On the contrary, he himself was losing ground, while Drona was taking immense toll of the Pandava army. Something needed to be done quickly.

Under such pressures, the Pandava camp decided to play a deceitful trick on Dronacharya. This deception was meant to make Drona vulnerable by demoralising him. And, it is said that this shameful strategy was conceived by none other than Krishna. Krishna presumably had said, "Oh Pandavas, leave alone anybody else, even Indra, the king of the gods, is incapable of defeating Drona in battle. But when he has discarded his weapons even a mere human being can kill him. So, go ahead and try to defeat him by making him want to discard his weapons even if you have to abuse your *Dharma*."

Strangely, only ten or twelve pages back, Krishna had said, "I vow to you that wherever Brahma, truth, restraint, purity, *Dharma*, majesty, modesty, mercy and patience dwell, there am I."

Further, Krishna had said that he descends on earth again and again, epoch after epoch, for the sole purpose of preserving *Dharma*. And so far in the *Mahabharata*, we have found him to be no one but a totally righteous person whose integrity of character even his enemies like Dhritarashtra have acknowledged. Was it possible for such a man to have seriously urged 'discard *Dharma*'? No wonder that one gets the impression of the *Mahabharata* being the work of many hands.

So, encouraging the Pandavas to play foul, Krishna had allegedly continued, "I strongly feel that if Drona hears that Asvatthama has been killed in battle, he will stop fighting. Somebody please go ahead and tell him that Asvatthama has succumbed to his injuries in combat."

Arjuna refused to lie. Yudhisthira half-heartedly agreed to it. Bhima, without wasting words, went and killed an elephant called Asvatthama. Then, he came to Drona and announced that Asvatthama had died. Drona knew how exceedingly brave and strong his son was and what a hurdle he was to his enemies. So he did not believe Bhima immediately but carried on with his job of attacking Dhristadyumna. Nevertheless, after a while, he took the trouble of asking Yudhisthira whether Bhima's words were true. As Yudhisthira never uttered a lie and always acted in favour of *Dharma*, Drona trusted him to tell the truth. Yudhisthira confirmed that the elephant, Asvatthama, had died but the words 'the elephant' remained inaudible.

The message distracted Drona for a few moments. But then, he enhanced his force of attack and had almost killed Dhristadyumna. Bhima hurried there and rescued his commander. Then, holding Drona's chariot, Bhima shouted to him a tirade of hurtful words. Among other accusations, Bhima damned Drona for acting like a *Chandala* by killing people indiscriminately, including even non-Aryan tribes. This violent act was quite unsuitable for a *Brahmin*, Bhima reminded him. Drona, Bhima complained, was being greedy for wealth and was only looking after the interest of his son and his wife.

Bhima's allegations did work, for basically Drona was a sensitive man. He stopped fighting and shed his weapons in shame. Soon Dhristadyumna appeared and beheaded him.

Now, let us systematically analyse whether the false announcement of Asvatthama's death really took place. Here, I request my readers to recall the methods I have put in place to examine the truth or falsity of any episode relating to Sri Krishna. According to one of my rules, whenever we find that the behaviour of a certain character is inconsistent with what he normally appears to be, we reject that behaviour as fabulous. For instance, if somewhere Bhima is depicted as a weakling, we would reject that portion as interpolated.

The false announcement of Asvatthama's death is inconsistent with the character of *Dharmatma* Yudhisthira who is reputed for his honesty.

It is also inconsistent with the character of Bhima who did not believe in using anything ever other than the strength of his own two hands. Above all, the falsehood is totally inconsistent with Krishna's character. If my readers have followed what I have pointed out so far in my work, they would know that falsehood is totally opposed to Krishna. It is as unrelated to him as light is to darkness, black is to white, heat is to coolness, gentility is to harshness, sickness is to health and friendship is to hatred.

When the incident of Asvatthama's death being falsely announced is inconsistent with not one but three basic characters of the *Mahabharata*, then it has to be a concocted one. We cannot accept it as the work of any principal poet of the *Mahabharata*.

My argument is not over yet. Examining with one method I have proved the story of the Pandavas faking Asvatthama's death as false. My second formula is to reject one account when any two accounts of the same event contradict each other. Now, besides the hearsay of a dead elephant playing a role in Drona's fall, we find another description of his last moments in the *Mahabharata*. This second account of Drona's death holds that when the *Acharya* was deeply engaged in battle, the sages Vishvamitra, Jamadagni, Vasistha, Atri, Bhrigu, Angira, Sikata, Prasni, Garga, Valakhilya, Maricipa and other lesser seers came to him and jointly urged him to desist from destroying his enemies by unscrupulous means. "You have committed a terrible crime," they said, "by using the *Brahmastra* on innocent people (civilians?) incapable of using any weapons."

Drona repented breaking the rules of war and contemplated ending his life. Soon Bhima arrived there and holding his chariot accused him of foul play. The intensity of Bhima's criticism devastated him completely. Sitting in a *yogasana* position, chanting the *Omkara* and praying to Vasudeva, the Lord of gods, he breathed his last. When he had died Dhristadyumna came and cut the head off the corpse.

My readers would notice that this description of Dronacharya's death is free from the strange announcement of Asvatthama's demise.

Which of the two accounts of Drona's end should we reject? Without any delay, we would reject the one with Asvatthama, the elephant, as it shows basic inconsistencies in the character-sketches of three main figures of the epic. Of course, the second description contains the fabulous account of several sages suddenly appearing on the battlefield. But this may simply be the poet's way of conveying that Drona had, in some way, broken the canons of war prevalent in those days. And Bhima's admonitions, in both the descriptions, support this.

Moreover, wherever else the mention of Drona's death appears in relation to other incidents of the *Mahabharata*, it is always without the alleged deceitful announcement.

Lastly, supposing that his son Asvatthama's death was really announced, would not Drona, before preparing to commit suicide on that account, thoroughly check out the authenticity of the news? Any sane person in Drona's place would do that.

I am so keen to prove my point in this particular case because Krishna has been most severely criticised (of course by people who believe him to be a human being and not a god) for this so-called foul play of his. His intimacy with the *gopis* is the only other issue that has brought him so much contempt over the ages.

But how did Drona really die? Perhaps he had broken some rules of war for which he was later remorseful. He could not have left the battleground even in that case for that would mean abandoning his patron, Duryodhana in his hour of need. It would also appear as a sign of his weakness. Embracing death, therefore, was perhaps his only way out. Perhaps this was the word-of-mouth information, which later became one of the building-blocks of the core story of the *Mahabharata*. Or, perhaps, Drona did not die in either of the two ways just related. Perhaps King Dhrupad's son Dhristadyumna had actually killed him in battle. Then, the authors of the *Mahabharata*, to absolve a prince of the powerful Panchala lineage from the sin of Brahminicide, had fabricated damage-controlling stories around it.

And why was Krishna made to be deceitful? As I explained in my earlier chapter, the author of this tract of the *Mahabharata* wanted to convey the idea that even untruth came from God.

◆

The Religion that Krishna Preached

The poet who conjured up the idea of misleading Drona with the false message of his son's death depicts Arjuna as the most honest person among the seniors of the Pandava camp. That Arjuna refused to lie where Yudhisthira, Bhima and Krishna did not, makes Arjuna's character appear superior to the others. However, what followed next considerably lowers his status as an ideal *Kshatriya* gentleman. There we find Arjuna acting like an idiot and a brute. And, we discover Krishna gently guiding him back to good behaviour. The following is how the author describes it:

After Drona, Karna had taken command of the Kaurava army. His daring had put the Pandavas in trouble. On one occasion, when Yudhisthira had to confront him, Karna had simply scared him away all the way to his own, personal camp-bed! Now, Arjuna, after a victorious encounter in another part of the battlefield, noticed that Yudhisthira was not around. Worried, he returned to camp and was relieved to find his eldest brother safe in bed. Yudhisthira was expecting to hear the news of Karna's fall from Arjuna, but on learning that Karna was still alive, burst into anger. He called Arjuna 'useless'. This was quite like the coward as he was, always expecting others to do for him the jobs he could not perform himself. Yudhisthira went on berating Arjuna until finally he said, "Give up your *Gandiva* (the name of Arjuna's personal bow). Let Krishna have it." Arjuna was too self-esteemed to tolerate such an insult even from his respected eldest brother. He unsheathed his sword to kill Yudhisthira saying, "It is my vow to slay anyone who calls me unworthy of *Gandiva*."

Krishna stopped him and, with gentle words, calmed him down. What he said to Arjuna explains Krishna's idea of religion. Krishna explained to Arjuna that **non-violence was the greatest principle of all. Observing non-violence was more important than keeping one's vow or telling the truth**. In other words, if a list of virtues was made, non-violence would have a higher place in it than truth. Other pious actions, like charity, austerity, devotion to God and maintaining cleanliness would follow the first two.

It is clear that strong arguments can be raised against Krishna's statements. Firstly, it is not practical to observe non-violence at all times. Secondly, Krishna himself, in the *Gita*, had motivated Arjuna towards violence.

The objections, however, would not arise if we understand the true meaning of non-violence. It is a fact of life that we cannot exist on earth even for a second without destroying living forms. We drink them with our drinking water, inhale them with the air we breathe in… cook them in our spinach and aubergine. All this we do even when we do not wish to be violent. Often we have to be violent willingly, like when we kill a poisonous snake. However, being violent **unnecessarily** is *Adharma*.

Krishna's passionate campaign for non-violence was strong enough to make Arjuna realise that it was unnecessary to kill his brother just to be true to his own words. However, would society at large, not Krishna alone, sanction Arjuna's vow-breaking?

In order to convince him that, even by the popular code of *Dharma*, Arjuna was not required to kill his brother to keep his vow, Krishna related how the society-elders viewed *Dharma*: "A pious person should speak the truth," the elders hold, "for there is nothing greater than the truth. However, where falsehood appears as truth and truth as falsehood, one is allowed to lie."

On the whole, Krishna had no disagreement with the established *Dharma* of his day. He, too, believed that truth and falsity, right and wrong depended on the situations they were linked to – what appeared to be true in one case might appear to be false in another case. And he also admitted that by applying specific guidelines given in the scriptures (*shrutis*) one could recognise what was *Dharma* and what was not. However, **Krishna put greater stress on one's personal discretion and**

lesser stress on blindly relying on religious dogma/guidelines given in the scriptures. He encouraged people to use their power of inference in deciding what *Dharma* **was.**

And Krishna said, "**What preserves life on earth is Dharma**". According to Krishna, a person had to, in the world around him, look for **signs** of what actually preserved life. Protecting those **signs** or **systems** was his primary *Dharma*.

In short, Krishna's religion was a form of utilitarianism, whose ultimate and practical aim was the safety and welfare of the human race.

✦

The Fall of Karna

Krishna was able to convince Arjuna that it was not necessary to kill his brother, Yudhisthira, just for the sake of honouring a vow. Nevertheless, a *Kshatriya* by birth and steeped in *Kshatriya* sensibilities, he was ever ready to give up his life for upholding a promise. He still felt uncomfortable for not keeping his words. Fortunately Krishna, again, had a solution for Arjuna's dilemma. He said, "Insulting an honourable man is as good as killing him. Go ahead, Arjuna, and slay your brother by slight." Arjuna did that but the next moment was overwhelmed with remorse. He was so ashamed of himself for humiliating his brother that he wanted to die. Krishna had a remedy for that ailment too. He said, "For a good man, boasting is like suicide." So Arjuna indulged in a lot of self-praise and his trouble was finally over.

We find that Krishna was more than Arjuna's charioteer. Quite often he was Arjuna's personal adviser and guide. On the battlefield, he was Arjuna's strategic consultant.

Returning from camp where they had gone in search of Yudhisthira, Krishna drove the chariot to where Karna was. He knew that the time was ripe for Arjuna to combat with the most important warrior on the Kaurava side.

The fall of Karna is a vital event of the *Mahabharata*. Over several chapters, the authors of the epic had carefully prepared the ground for this great climax. Karna, who had an outstanding record as a warrior, was Arjuna's arch-rival. The glory and prosperity he had gained single-handed for Duryodhana was no less than what the four younger brothers of Yudhisthira had won for him collectively. Where Arjuna was the disciple of Drona, Karna was the disciple of Drona's guru, Parashurama. Arjuna was famous for his *Gandiva* bow, Karna was famous for his *Vijaya* bow, a better weapon than the *Gandiva*. Where Krishna was Arjuna's charioteer, the immensely brave Shalya was Karna's. Both Karna and Arjuna had vowed to kill each other. Arjuna was quite casual in his approach to felling Bhishma and Drona. For slaying Karna, his determination was at its peak. In the past when Kunti, after revealing that she was his mother, had begged for the lives of her five other sons, Karna had promised to spare them all except Arjuna. He had predicted that he would kill Arjuna or be killed by him.

Krishna was taking Arjuna for that long-awaited critical encounter. In fact, it was a ploy of Krishna to have brought Arjuna to the camp looking for Yudhisthira. Arjuna was not at all keen on leaving the battleground. It was Krishna who had made an excuse out of Yudhisthira's absence in the field in order to persuade Arjuna to take a break from active encounter. Refreshed, he would have an edge over Karna who was fighting continuously. Further, to motivate Arjuna for defeating Karna, on their journey back to the battlefield, Krishna praised him highly for all his glorious achievements. He also reminded him of how Karna had tortured the Pandavas, especially by slaying young Abhimanyu and by insulting Draupadi.

Without going into the details of Krishna's speech on that occasion, I must point out to my readers one interesting fact. It is that throughout his delivery Krishna used such phrases as 'the way Vishnu killed the *Danavas* in mythology', 'when the *Danavas* got killed by Vishnu', etc., indicating that Krishna was addressing Vishnu as another being, not himself. There is no doubt that this tract is from the core *Mahabharata* where Krishna was not yet considered to be an incarnation of Vishnu.

Soon the two rivals, Karna and Arjuna, faced each other. In the course of that terrible battle, Karna's serpent arrow was about to strike Arjuna. Krishna, with his quick footwork, depressed the chariot into the ground so that only the tip of Arjuna's headgear broke off. This, with many other examples in the *Mahabharata*, proves Krishna's excellence as a charioteer.

Towards the end of the battle, a wheel of Karna's chariot got jammed into the ground. Karna needed to get down to free the wheel. Arjuna allowed him to do so, for, as per the rules of war, he was not supposed to strike his opponent until his vehicle was on the move again. Unfortunately for Karna, he did not take Arjuna's sense of duty for granted and reminded him that Arjuna was **under obligation** to spare him while he was retrieving the wheel.

This gave tactful Krishna an opportunity to remind Karna of all the negligence of duty he, Karna, had committed in his life. This Krishna did to demoralise Karna and to prompt Arjuna to kill him without delay. Insulting Draupadi, being party to a fraudulent dice game, advising Duryodhana to poison Bhima, trying to burn the Pandavas alive when they were living in *Varanavata*, being one of the warriors who overpowered Abhimanyu to death — were all sinful acts of Karna. After committing so much *Adharma* himself, did Karna deserve to be treated kindly just because he was having some problem with his chariot-wheel, Krishna demanded. This left Karna speechless and full of remorse. When the battle resumed, Karna seemed to have lost interest in it and was soon killed by Arjuna's arrows.

The Fall of Duryodhana

After Karna fell, Duryodhana made Shalya his General.

In the previous day's war, Yudhisthira had shown cowardice by running away from the battlefield. He needed to do something brave now to redeem his self-esteem. Krishna, wisely, made him face Shalya, the Supreme Commander of the opposition. Yudhisthira, too, rising up to the occasion, fought courageously and claimed his opponent's life.

That day, except the *Brahmins* Kripa and Asvatthama, the Yadava Kritavarma and Duryodhana himself, the entire Kaurava army was wiped out by the Pandavas. Looking for Duryodhana, the Pandavas found him hiding in Lake Dvaipayana. But the Pandavas hesitated to kill him without a fight. King Yudhisthira, especially, was too fair-minded to take advantage of the situation. However, Yudhisthira's extreme fascination for justice often made him act impractically. In the present case, he suddenly had a brainwave. He invited Duryodhana to choose any one warrior among the Pandava brothers to fight a duel with him using any weapon of his (Duryodhana's) liking. If he won the battle, Yudhisthira promised, Duryodhana would get his kingdom back.

Duryodhana declared that he would fight with a mace. And, with a nonchalant stance typical of a warring Kshatriya of his time, asked any Pandava to confront him. Fortunately, Bhima came forward to face him. In case Duryodhana had chosen somebody other than Bhima for a mace-fight, he was sure to have won, for only Bhima was up to Duryodhana's calibre in the use of that weapon. And that would have undone whatever the Pandavas had gained in the great *Mahabharata* war so far. In a clear-cut manner, Krishna pointed this out to Yudhisthira and severely criticised him for his awkward decisions.

At this point, a sudden change takes over the characterisation of the central figures of the *Mahabharata*. And, we find its main personalities noticeably deviating from their basic nature depicted so far.

In the past eighteen days' war, Bhima and Duryodhana had often attacked each other with their maces and every time Bhima had won. On the last day, however, Duryodhana was praised as being the superior of the two! It is said that in their final encounter Bhima was on the brink of a dismal defeat. My guess is that in this case, the author was forced to make Duryodhana a more accomplished rival as he wanted to link their duel with a terrible vow Bhima had taken.

After the Pandavas were defeated in a fraudulent dice game, Duryodhana had insulted Draupadi by showing her his bare thigh. Bhima, in his anger, had vowed to break that thigh as soon as he got the opportunity. Now, the opportunity had come. The two stalwarts were engaged in a confrontation with their favourite weapons. Bhima, obviously, would try his best to break his opponent's thigh. The only hurdle was that, according to the rules of a mace-fight, a contestant could not hit his adversary below the navel. So, the author had no option but to make Bhima defeat Duryodhana by breaking rules. The scene is related in the following way:

After watching Bhima and Duryodhana's duel, Arjuna asked Krishna, "Who, do you think, is the better of the two?"

Krishna replied, "Bhima, no doubt, is physically stronger. But Duryodhana has passion and better technique. And now that he is desperate for his life, he can win. It would be impossible for Bhima to defeat Duryodhana unless he plays foul."

Hearing this, Arjuna slapped his own left thigh for Bhima to see. The hint reminded Bhima of his famous vow and he struck Duryodhana on the thigh according to his oath.

It is clear that the author of this tract of the *Mahabharata* adjusts the plot in the way he does, to accommodate Bhima's fulfilment of his vow. However, while doing so, he produces several inconsistencies in characterisation. It was quite unlike Bhima to forget his vow and quite unlike Arjuna, who had refused to lie even to make Drona fall, to encourage Bhima to fight unfairly. And it seems the composer deliberately establishes Krishna as unfair by making him the supplier of the idea of cheating. Not only that, he defames Krishna by making him taunt the dying Duryodhana a little while later! This is quite in opposition to the calm and composed bearing in which Krishna is generally presented.

His thigh badly broken, Duryodhana knew he was going to die soon. He told his enemies, "I have achieved a *Kshatriya's* honourable end by dying in a war. I will go to heaven with my brothers, other relatives and friends. With your hearts filled with grief, you will be left discarded on earth."

There is nothing unusual in the above statement. Any vanquished person as conceited as Duryodhana would use such expression at the moment of his death to say that he had won, after all. However, what is surprising is the reaction to his death. The poet describes the passing away of Duryodhana by saying, "Petals of flowers rained from the sky. The *Gandharvas* played music. The *Apsaras* sang Duryodhana's praises. The ascetics spoke of his goodness. The atmosphere grew pure and calm.... Watching all this, Krishna and the Pandavas were ashamed of their misdeeds."

It is unbelievable that the person who is described as a sinful villain throughout the *Mahabharata* would be suddenly praised so much. It is also difficult to believe that the heroes of the epic well known for their honesty and forthrightness should be ashamed of their 'misdeeds'. These contradictions are surprising, for they oppose the basic scheme of the *Mahabharata*. The main theme of the epic is to commend the righteous Krishna-Pandavas against the wrong-doer Duryodhana.

The queer passage describing the scene of Duryodhana's death does not merit any discussion. My intention for bringing it up was to show what peculiar things Sanskrit books might contain. Yet many of my unfortunate countrymen believe that the contents of any Sanskrit book are the words of seers and need to be blindly accepted.

It is needless to say that the passage in context is unoriginal. And it does not even bear the mark of the type two poet of the *Mahabharata*. For, I find that the author of the second layer of the *Mahabharata* is a devotee of Krishna whereas in the fall of Duryodhana, **Krishna is belittled and blamed again and again**. This chapter, I feel, must belong to the third layer of the *Mahabharata*. Shaivaites and other Vaishnava-haters have contributed to the *Mahabharata* from time to time. The verses relating to Duryodhana's death might have come from one of them. Yet, I cannot be fully sure of that conclusion for Hindu poets have been found, at times, singing praises of their heroes in the guise of abuse. This could be an example of that technique – a reverse euphemism! In any case, we find Duryodhana confiding in Asvatthama just before he died, "I am quite aware of the greatness of Vasudeva. He has not led me astray..."

So we find that the opus of the *Mahabharata*, open to contributions from many sources for a long period of time, makes a truly critical analysis of it extremely difficult.

◆

The Last Days of the War

Before he died, Duryodhana made Asvatthama his Supreme Commander. However, by then, the Kaurava army consisted only of himself (Asvatthama), Kripacharya and Kritavarma.

Gandhari's piety had earned for her some extraordinary powers. And Yudhisthira feared that if she willed she could reduce the Pandavas to ashes for slaying Duryodhana by unfair means. He, therefore, requested Krishna to make a special visit to her and her husband Dhritarashtra to placate them. The section describing Yudhisthira's request to Krishna, clearly does not belong to the core *Mahabharata* because there we find Yudhisthira addressing Krishna as, "You are unchangeable, and you are the Lord of all creation…"

The war of Kurukshetra ended with a terrible nocturnal attack. One night Asvatthama sneaked into the Pandava camp and slayed the sleeping Pandava heroes Dhristadyumna, Sikhandi and Draupadi's five sons. He also killed the soldiers of all the other army units of the Pandavas along with their leaders and every member of the Panchala family.

When the war ended, the widows of the fallen heroes went into mourning. Such heartrending cries of grief had never ever been heard! About Krishna, two important things have been said in the section describing the end of the war:

Dhritarashtra – 'who had the physical prowess of a million elephants' – had planned to shatter Bhima to death when he embraced him. Foreseeing that, Krishna had arranged for an iron statue of Bhima.

He made the blind king break that statue believing it to be Bhima. We can easily consider this incident as completely mythical.

Gandhari in her distress accused Krishna of destroying both the Kaurava and the Pandava households. And she bestowed a curse on him by which all the households of the Yadava clan would also be similarly destroyed after thirty-six years. (How strange that it would be after exactly thirty six years!) And that an heirless, friendless Krishna wandering in the forests would meet an ugly death.

It is said that Krishna had smilingly replied, "Oh adorable one! You have just said what exactly is going to happen. The Yadavas cannot be destroyed by gods, *Danavas* or humans. But fate decrees that they would destroy themselves. There is no doubt that they would annihilate one another."

In the above manner, the poet of the second stratum of the *Mahabharata* prepares the ground for his chapter on *Maushala* which describes the Yadava ruin.

Setting up a Legislation

We have come to the end of our bumpy ride through the Kurukshetra war. Once again we are on smooth ground. And where Krishna is concerned, his character is again unblemished and chaste. In fact, in *Shanti Parva* and *Anushasana Parva*, Krishna's virtue and piety is so highly exaggerated that he acquires the status of near divinity.

When the war had ended His Highness, the supremely wise Yudhisthira, took another infinitely wise step! Relating to Arjuna how wretched he felt after killing his own relatives, he declared that he wanted to live a beggar's life in the forests. Arjuna was irritated with Yudhisthira's attitude, of his not appreciating what a tough job winning the war was. He strongly disagreed with the idea of leaving everything behind and going to the forests again. However, even after Bhima, Nakula, Sahadeva, Draupadi and Krishna argued with Yudhisthira to make him realise what a silly thought he had got, Yudhisthira's mind was set. The sages Vyasa and Narada as well as some other famous personalities came to persuade Yudhisthira to change his mind but all failed. It was Krishna, at last, who was able to convince him to enjoy victory. And, finally, he entered Hastinapura a very jubilant man indeed.

Krishna coroneted Yudhisthira as king. Yudhisthira eulogised Krishna and bowed to him. Krishna was younger to Yudhisthira in years. As such, it was unusual for the latter to salute the former in that manner. And, we never found him doing so earlier.

At that time, the great Kaurava hero, Bhishma, was lying yet on his deathbed of arrows. Stoically bearing his physical pain, he was waiting to die at the auspicious hour of summer solstice. Bhishma and the sages who stood around his deathbed prayed to 'Almighty' Krishna. Moved by their prayers, Krishna arrived there with Yudhisthira and his companions. On their way to meet Bhishma, Yudhisthira had humbly urged Krishna to tell them the story of Parashurama. Krishna obliged.

Then Krishna advised Yudhisthira to receive lessons from Bhishma. Bhishma possessed the knowledge of all types of *Dharmas*. Krishna's intension was that it should not be lost with his death. Coming to Bhishma's bedside, Krishna urged him (Bhishma) to instruct Yudhisthira. But Bhishma said, "You yourself are the source of all knowledge and all action. You should be the one teaching Yudhisthira. I am in great pain and am mentally disoriented. I am not fit enough to speak clearly." Krishna said, "I reward you with a boon which will liberate you from pain... your mind will stay sharp... you will be able to see the past, the future and everything else that can be conceived beyond that."

Bhishma immediately received all the special abilities promised to him by Krishna. Yet he was still reluctant to preach *Dharma*. "Why don't you teach Yudhisthira yourself, my Lord?" he asked. Krishna said, "It is true that I am the source of all creation and know everything about it. But I want my glory to shine forth. It shall be fulfilled by that just as the moon is fulfilled when it radiates its cool rays. I want to make you immensely illustrious by extending my wisdom to you."

Bhishma, then, cheerfully related all the intricacies and subtleties of *Dharma* to Yudhisthira. *Shanti Parva* ends here.

All the three strata of the *Mahabharata* are represented in this chapter. The first layer is present there in its skeletal form. And then, the nature of *Dharma* is explained by different authors according to individual understanding of it, forming the other two layers. From what is related in this chapter, we must take note of one important issue. Implicit in whatever is being said here is the understanding that crowning a conscientious ruler is not equivalent to establishing a *Dharma Rajya*. Fair-minded Yudhisthira would not live forever. His heir could turn out to be an unfair ruler. Therefore, the enthroning of a righteous king should be followed by encoding a structure of rules, based on *Dharma*, to be followed even after his death. Winning a war was only the first step of establishing any kingdom. The next, more important step, was to establish a system of right governance. We find that Krishna chose

Bhishma to formulate that set of rules. And he had valid reasons to nominate him for this. "You are a senior person of good conduct and great learning. You know all the duties and responsibilities of a ruler and the duties and responsibilities of people in other positions..." Krishna had said.

◆

Sermons on Desire

When Bhishma was no more, Yudhisthira once again drowned himself in tears. Again, he made a big fuss about going to the forests. This time Krishna confronted him squarely. He knew, better than anybody else, what exactly was the problem with Yudhisthira. What troubled Yudhisthira was his own ego. He was distracted and disturbed by his own muddled self. Deeply subjective issues like 'I have committed sin', 'I am distressed' etc were at the root of all his lamentations.

Krishna hit at that root by gravely declaring, "You have enemies left to kill yet — enemies that are within your own being. Oh righteous king, there are two types of illnesses in this world — physical and mental — of whom each support the other. Phlegm, bile and wind are elements of the body and should be in harmony to keep the body healthy. Similarly, virtue, passion and disgust, the elements of human feelings, have to maintain balance to keep the mind healthy…. At this moment, you have to keep up your mental balance. Do not drown yourself in sorrow. Do not be too jubilant. Be objective. Banish your personal desires, and with a steady heart, rule your ancestral province righteously.

"Now, please listen to me as I describe the nature of desire in the style of the learned ones: Desire itself says, 'No one can conquer me without detachment and discipline. When someone tries to win me over by prayers, I settle in his mind as conceit and spoil his work. When someone wants to dispel me in order to acquire eternal salvation, I laugh at him tauntingly. No wonder the learned call me mind-boggling and indestructible.'

"So, you see, *Dharmaraja*, that desire can never be abandoned. Better to direct your desires towards doing good by performing *Ashwamedha* and other important *Yajnas*. Your desire that your friends who have died would come back to you would never be fulfilled. So do not get overwhelmed repeatedly by it. Achieve something fruitful on earth by performing the great *Yajnas*. That would be of benefit to you even in your next life."

Last Meeting with the Pandavas

Dharma Rajya had been established. *Dharma* had been preached. This book of mine refers to the Pandavas only because of their relationship with Krishna. And, Krishna appears in the *Mahabharata* by dint of his relationship with the Pandavas. Now, Krishna's role in the *Mahabharata* being over, he needs his exeunt. However, the zealous authors of the *Mahabharata* (like the news-hunters of today) would not leave him easily.

They ploy Krishna to stay by having Arjuna make an absurd request, "I have forgotten all that you taught me about *Dharma* before the war. Will you, please, teach it to me again?" To this Krishna says, "It's quite unfortunate that you've forgotten my lessons, for those words would not occur to me again. At the time of the war, I was under the spell of special powers. Moreover, now that I find you had barely paid attention to my speeches, I have no intention of instructing you any more. Nevertheless, here is an ancient story…"

Relating a long story of an ancient personality, Krishna taught some more lessons to Arjuna. What Krishna had taught Arjuna previously is famously known as the *Gita*. What Krishna taught Arjuna the second time has been called the *Anugita* (the minor *Gita*) by its author. A part of the *Anugita* is called the *Brahmagita*.

In fact we find that several discourses on *Dharma*, namely, the *Bhagavata Gita*, the *Prajagara*, the *Sanata Sullajja*, the *Markandeya Samasya* etc along with the *Anugita* are included in the *Mahabharata* and have become its valuable inseparable parts. Among the above books, the *Gita* (the *Bhagavata Gita*) has the primary position as a religious tome.

Even so, the others, including the *Anugita*, carry important messages. Prof. Max Muller has included the *Anugita* in his work *The Sacred Books of the East*. And, Sri Kasinath Trambak Telang, a judge in Bombay High Court, has translated it into English. However, as Kasinath says and proves conclusively in the introduction of his commendable work, the teachings of the *Anugita* cannot be the teachings of Krishna. In fact, it can be firmly established that the *Anugita* was conceived centuries after the composition of the original *Gita*.

To continue with our story of the *Mahabharata*, after imparting his lessons to Arjuna the second time, Krishna took leave of him and Yudhisthira. Then, he went back to Dwaraka. His leave-taking is described as an emotional parting of friends.

On reaching Dwaraka, Krishna met with his peers and relatives. His father Vasudeva wanted to hear the account of the Kurukshetra war from him. Krishna gave him a condensed version. This version is bereft of any unnatural or supernatural event or any exaggeration. However, all the important episodes, except Abhimanyu's death, were included in his report. It was Abhimanyu's mother Subhadra (who was also in Dwaraka at that time) who was the first to report that tragedy. So, Krishna gave his father a gist of that sad incident too.

When parting from Krishna, Yudhisthira had invited him to grace the occasion of the *Ashwamedha Yajna* he was about to perform. So, as soon as that programme was fixed, Krishna was in Hastinapura again, with many other Yadavas. It is said that on that trip, Krishna brought to life Abhimanyu's widow Uttara's stillborn son. But that does not prove that Krishna had superhuman powers. Today, many doctors can revive newborns who are apparently dead. And how that can be done is a known medical procedure. Krishna, could have had learnt the rare skill of assisting such births. No wonder he was known to be an outstanding all-rounder of his time.

The *Yajna* over, Krishna returned to Dwaraka. He and the Pandavas never met ever again.

✦

Section - VII
The Incidents in Prabhasha

Annihilation of the Yadus

*N*ow we describe the *Maushala Parva* where Krishna and Balarama pass away and the entire Yadava clan is exterminated. Krishna did nothing to prevent the pathetic end of the Yadavas. On the contrary, he himself slaughtered many of them. The last days of the Yadavas have been recorded in the following manner:

As Gandhari had predicted, exactly thirty-six years after she had cursed the Yadavas, the clan was falling apart due to appalling degeneration of their moral values. While they were in such a quandary, the renowned sages Vishvamitra, Kanva and Narada visited them. A group of profligate Yadavas brought Krishna's son Shamba disguised as a woman to the sages. And the silly Yadavas asked the sages, "This lady, here, is expecting a child. Will she give birth to a boy?"

In our *Puranas* and *Itihasas*, many sages are shown to possess explosive temper. Slight provocations would make them pronounce terrifying curses. I wonder why they were said to be, 'the conquerors of the senses' and 'the devotees of God'. According to me, they should have been ranked among the cruellest monsters in human shapes! In today's world, most gentlemen would laugh at the poor joke the Yadava lads were trying to make. Or may be they would get annoyed and pass some critical but generally harmless comments. Not so the sages of ancient India! Upset at the Yadavas' behaviour (of asking the venerable sages a silly question), they instantly cursed the whole Yadu clan. "That woman will give birth to an iron pestle by which all the Yadus, except Krishna and Balarama will be destroyed," they predicted.

When Krishna heard about the terrible curse he made no effort to reverse it. "The sages' wish will be fulfilled," he said passively.

In due course of time, Shamba (though a man) gave birth to an iron pestle or club. Ugrasena, the king of the Yadavas, to alleviate the ill-omen, got it finely pounded and the dust thrown into the sea. By that time, the Yadavas' morality had worsened. Krishna, fed up with them, wished for their total destruction. Wanting them to die, he sent them to the pilgrimage of Prabhasha. (Was it auspicious to die in a holy place?)

In Prabhasha, the Yadavas drank and made merry for some time. Then they began to quarrel. The great hero of Kurukshetra war, Satyaki, was the one who started the fight. Pradyumna joined him in his conflict with Kritavarma. Soon Satyaki beheaded Kritavarma. Kritavarma's family members, in return, killed both Satyaki and Pradyumna.

The trouble was that the Yadavas were divided into many sub-clans which disagreed with one another on important issues. During the outing at *Prabhasha*, where Krishna had joined them, he was sick of their petty wrangles. Then he began to kill his own people with *ekara* reeds. Legend has it that the reeds Krishna used to kill the Yadavas had actually grown out of the iron dust made from pulverising the pestle that Shamba had given birth to. It is also said that all the *ekara* reeds of that area had turned into pestles with which the Yadavas killed one another.

Soon Krishna sent his charioteer Daruka to Hastinapura with the errand to bring Arjuna. He wanted Arjuna to take charge of the Yadava women and chaperon them away from strife-torn Dwaraka.

In the meantime, Balarama, not wishing to live a moment longer, gave up his life. This saddened Krishna so much that he too desired to die. While he was lying on the ground, dejected, a hunter named Jara, mistaking his feet as the part of a deer's body struck them with his arrows.... Gently consoling Jara for his blunder, Krishna breathed his last.

When Arjuna reached Dwaraka, both Krishna and Balarama had died. He performed their last rites before leaving for Hastinapura with the Yadava housewives and girls. On their way, they were attacked by a band of vandals armed with staff. The great Arjuna, who had killed

Bhishma and Karna in the past, on this occasion failed to fight even a group of cudgel-holding village louts.[6] Except Rukmini, Satyabhama, Haimavati, Jambuvati and a few other principal ladies, the women could not be saved. They were all carried away by the raiders.

No doubt that the events surrounding the Yadavas' annihilation are mostly fictitious. However, the foundations on which the stories were built are basically true. For example, some facts about the Yadavas are well-established. Their excessive drinking of alcohol has been mentioned elsewhere. (It is said that their excessive drinking had once led Krishna and Balarama to declare that anyone producing liquor would be put to death.) It is also known that the Yadava clan constituted of many sub-clans and family groups.

These small groups frequently disagreed with one another on important issues. In the *Mahabharata* war, Krishna and Satyaki of the Varshneya sub-clan had joined the Pandavas, while Kritavarma of the Bhoja family had joined the Kauravas. Moreover, the Yadavas did not have a proper ruler or sovereign to govern them. Even though Ugrasena is sometimes addressed as 'king', it is well-known that he was not the supreme commander of his people.

Krishna was an important leader of the Yadavas by dint of his personal capabilities, but his ideas and opinions often differed even from his own elder brother Balarama. It is given in the *Shanti Parva* of the *Mahabharata* what Krishna revealed to Sage Narada about his frustrations with his kinsmen. There, Krishna had related how even after his most sincere efforts to please his people, he had been unable to make them happy with him.

In short, the Yadavas were, at the time we are referring to, querulous, free-thinking, energetic people who had taken to excessive drinking and had fallen into immoral habits. These potentially dangerous defects had probably ruined the Yadavas. Krishna and Balarama probably had died in the broil itself or disappointed with their fate, had committed suicide. Folklore built upon the events must have given rise to the improbable stories.

---

[6] *Translator's Footnote*
It is stated in the *Vishnu Purana* that Krishna lived for more than a hundred years. As Krishna's contemporary, Arjuna must have been a frail, old man when the above encounter took place.

What concerns us about the Yadavas' annihilation, though, is Krishna's role in it. It is recorded that Krishna did nothing to save his clan, that, in fact, he assisted the process of destruction by slaying many of its members.

I find nothing dishonourable or inconsistent in Krishna's character for his active participation in the Yadavas' demolition. Krishna was dutiful. It became Krishna's duty to destroy the Yadavas when they were perverted. He had killed Jarasandha and other evil people. If he did not kill the Yadavas when they were wicked, he would fail as a follower of *Dharma* and would be committing the crime of nepotism. An ideal person cannot do that and Krishna desisted from doing that.

Exactly how Krishna died remains somewhat vague. Four suggestions can be forwarded regarding the cause of his death:

That he was killed by the jealous Yadavas like Julius Caesar was killed by his friends. A group of scholars, led by Talboys and Wheeler, has this opinion. We have no proof, though, to support this view.

That he resorted to Yoga and willingly left his mortal body. Disciples of Western scientists would not believe that death could occur in this manner. I personally find no cause for disbelief in this case. People who have practised holding their breaths for a long time may hold their breaths until death. Suicide is considered to be a crime. But perhaps no sin can be attached to an elderly person's willing union with God after he has led a long and meritorious life.

That he died by the hunter Jara's arrows.

It is stated in the *Vishnu Purana* that Krishna lived over a hundred years. Maybe he just died of old age.

My readers who have come to believe that Krishna was a human being and not a divine incarnation can accept any of the four possible reasons of his death. **However, I am a believer. I accept that Krishna was divine. I insist that Krishna's feats on this earth had never crossed the limits of human abilities. But, according to me, he had contained himself within those limits only, because he wished his life to be an example for flesh-and-blood human beings, not superhuman beings.**

As an incarnation of God, he could still time his own birth and death on earth according to his own wish.[7]

In my opinion, the chapter on Yadavas' destruction is a later addition. Only what Krishna had done in connection with the Pandavas is given in the *Mahabharata*. Other than that, no account of Krishna is found in the epic, except what the last section carries. Moreover, Krishna here is described as God's incarnation which itself is a sign of a later strata of the *Mahabharata*.

✦

---

[7] *Translator's Footnote*
The passage, highlighted by the translator, seems to dent all the arguments given in Bankim's thesis so far. Bankim has painstakingly proved how human Krishna was. One would suppose that he really believed Krishna to be a human being. But one finds that he still endorses him as a divine incarnation. It is interesting to note how faith can influence even the most logical and scientific of human minds.

Conclusion

A critic's work on Krishna must be arranged into two divisions:
1. Demolishing the age-old myths surrounding his life
2. Reconstructing the truth about him

In my work on Krishna, my energy was principally directed towards dispelling the myths. Reconstructing the whole truth about him would be an extremely difficult proposition. For, the ashes of falsehood have covered the fire of truth. The elements with which I could build Krishna anew have sunk into the sea of lies. I did the reconstruction as best as I could.

In this concluding chapter, it is my duty to examine how does the truth, however little it might be, found in the *Puranas* and *Itihasas*, portray Krishna's personality.

We find that Krishna had great physical strength since his childhood. He had protected the people of Vrindavana from ferocious beasts. He had killed the wrestlers of Kansa. He could outrun Kalyavana. He was an outstanding charioteer.

Krishna had sharpened his natural physical abilities with training. In the use of weapons, his skill was better than most of the *Kshatriyas* of his time. Nobody could subdue him. He had defeated Kansa, Jarasandha, Shishupala and several other great warriors including the rulers of Varanasi, Kalinga, Paundrik and Gandhara. Krishna's disciples in the subject of warfare – Satyaki and Abhimanyu – were almost invincible. Even Arjuna had taken lessons on weaponry from Krishna.

Descriptions of war in the *Puranas* and the *Itihasas* give account of strength and bravery of its heroes but hardly deal with leadership qualities. It seems that strategic thinking was not a great asset of the warriors of our past. Neither Bhima nor Arjuna is praised for foresight. In his time, only Krishna stands out for having a sublime genius for planning. Because of his able leadership qualities and proper foresight, a light Yadava army could win over the mighty forces of Jarasandha. It was, again, Krishna's prophetic vision that made the Yadava clan migrate to Dwaraka in Raivataka.

Krishna had a phenomenal capacity to learn. The religion he preached gives evidence of his scholarly bent of mind. The *Gita* carries almost superhuman wisdom. Krishna's knowledge of statesmanship was also praiseworthy. Yudhisthira valued Krishna's advice above all others. Krishna excelled in several branches of knowledge – philosophy, religion, medicine, music and even horse-keeping.

Krishna was down-to-earth and practical, brave and quick-witted. He worked tirelessly at whatever needed to be done.

He was unwaveringly devoted to truth and *Dharma*. He had kindness and goodwill for all. My analysis of his life has convinced me of Krishna's exceptional goodness. Even though he was superior in physical strength to many mighty, conceited heroes of his time, he was determined to bring about universal peace and made sincere efforts to achieve it. He was kind even to the cows and other animals. He had stopped the worship of Indra and encouraged the Yadavas to take care of the animals in their habitat.

We have known Krishna to be a well-wisher of his clan. And yet, when any of his relatives acted sinfully, Krishna vehemently opposed them. We have seen how forgiving Krishna was and yet, when the time came for him to deliver punishment, how he could steel his heart and how unhesitating he could be in his judgement.

Thus, we find that many a noble quality had flourished in Krishna's character. However, that did not cause him to neglect the finer arts. I have not discussed this side of Krishna in detail but we know that he was a charming entertainer in Vrindavana. In later years, he spent many joyous hours in the sea and river cruises in the hill resort of Raivataka. This enchanting side of him contributed to making him the magnificent all-rounder that he undoubtedly was.

Only one important element seems to be missing in Krishna's character. I have explained in my book, *Dharmatatva,* that the sentiment of devotion is the noblest of all human feelings. Where do we find Krishna's devotion or *Bhakti*? In the *Mahabharata,* Krishna is sometimes described as the devotee of Shiva. However, all such passages seem to be interpolated.

I imagine that Krishna's object of devotion was himself. Devotion for oneself can come only to someone who can be convinced that there is no separation between himself and the creator. This conviction is thought to be the ultimate attainment of *Jnanamarga* (path of knowledge). This attainment is called *Atmarati* (bliss in one's supreme self). In the *Chhandogya Upanishad, Atmarati* is defined in the following way:

"He who has seen this, realised this, known this, has acted with this, has made this his partner, who has enjoyed this 'Self' is the Lord."

The *Gita* reveals that Krishna was such an '*Atmarama*', the knower of the Self, the Self that is the Universe. I cannot explain the meaning of *Atmarama*[8] more clearly than this.

To conclude, we find Krishna to be a bright example of a complete man. He was unconquered and unconquerable. He was pure-hearted, virtuous, loving, kind, dutiful, a follower of *Dharma*, a Vedic scholar, a master of ethics, someone who had only goodwill for the human race, who was just, merciful, impartial but also one who did not hesitate to punish the punishable. Krishna was not possessive in his attitude. He was humble, disciplined and dedicated like a yogi. Krishna functioned like a human being within the limits of human abilities but his inborn genius raised him to superhuman status. Through his superhuman abilities, he rose towards godliness.

---

[8] *Translator's Footnote*
However, that the sentiment of *Bhakti* was not regarded as a supreme quality in a human character during the time of the *Mahabharata* and had gained significance in India much later is a well-established fact now. Naturally, Bankim found *Bhakti* missing from Krishna's character. On the other hand, when Bankim lived, *Bhakti* was thought to be, especially in Bengal, a great mark of nobility in a person. So, Bankim seems to have, intelligently, defined Krishna an *Atmarama* (one who has supreme bliss in himself).

Whether Krishna was a god or a human being is to be judged by every individual reader of my thesis according to his or her way of thinking. My readers who decide that Krishna was but a man can call him what Rhys Davids had called the Buddha: "The wisest and the greatest of the Hindus."

My other readers who feel that Krishna had the signs of being divine may join me in humbly reciting the ending lines of my work: "The supreme being that is embodied here... is not restricted by the laws of the earth."

Translator's Epilogue

About two hundred years after Krishna died, he was made into a full-fledged god. The crude villagers who had vandalised the women of Dwaraka moving to Hastinapura with Arjuna, were of the Abhira community who kept cows like the Yadavas, even though they were not *Kshatriyas*. Luckily for them, however, in the next few decades, they gained a considerable measure of economic and political power and established their kingdoms in Western India. Like all other newly-come rulers of our country, they soon wanted to upgrade their caste. They took the title of Yadava as the Yadavas were milkmen like them but belonged to the *Kshatriya* caste. They made Krishna, a cowherd, their god. Stories of child Krishna stealing butter, playing pranks and making love to the *gopis* were colourfully retold. The anecdotes, then, became profoundly popular throughout the country.

♦

Translator's Note A

The Mahabharata and its Time

The core narrative of the *Mahabharata* was in existence as early as around 1500 BC. By then, the Aryans who had came to India had subordinated their native foes. Victory was conclusive. Now, it was time to divide among themselves what the members of the tribe had gained collectively and to rule their territory successfully. Such existential problems needed systems and laws of regulating society and keeping down internal strife. While the Greek City States had structured their polity by dividing the community into compartments of Senators, Freemen, Women and Slaves, ancient India's Aryans used the Caste System (see next note). However, at the same time, they also acknowledged the contribution of every individual's personal judgement in the efficient workings of the society. It was thought that if individuals were conscientious at personal levels, it would benefit the community as a whole. Thus arose the conception of *Dharma*. *Dharma* meant the true path or the path of righteousness. It was propounded that anyone who followed *Dharma*, however lowly he may be, would progress towards the ultimate goal – the *summum bonum* of earthly existence – the Absolute Salvation (*Moksha*).

Keeping one's word or vow was also *Dharma*.

At the time of the *Mahabharata*, people who mattered – and especially the *Kshatriyas* – were proud and headstrong. In the cultural milieu of the early years of human civilisation, when physical strength was needed all the time to protect society from falling apart, it was but natural that people would be so. When hurt, angered or defeated, the quick-tempered people of the *Mahabharata* would often curse or take vows of revenge on an impulse. Then, often, whole lives would be spent in fulfilling those promises.

To complicate matters, the *Dharma* of one individual would often clash with another's or many other individuals'. To quote from the *Mahabharata*: 'Different are the *Vedas*, different are the *Smritis*. Every *savant* has a different view. *Dharma's* essence is hidden in a cave of ignorance. So, the right path is to follow the righteous supermen.' No wonder that even the leaders of the society were at a loss and often in disagreement as to how to guide their followers. Many such cross-currents keep the tempo of the story of the *Mahabharata* charged from the beginning to the end.

◆

Translator's Note B

The Caste System in India

The word 'caste' is equivalent to the Sanskrit word *jati* and not *varna*. The word comes from Portuguese *casta* meaning breed, race or kind. The *varnas*, on the other hand, were the four classes of people into which Rig Vedic society was divided – *Brahmin, Kshatriya, Vaishya* and *Shudra*, below which were the outcastes.

What we understand as caste system of India is a system of many smaller units within the four broad divisions of *varnas* and the outcastes. The social customs by which a caste lives are usually different in several respects from those of other castes. A person of one caste is not supposed to marry into another. It is estimated that at present there are approximately 3000 castes in India.

It is generally supposed that *'Chatur Varna'* means the four colours. It is not so. *Varna* in this context does not mean colour. In Sanskrit, the word *varna* is derived from the root *vr* or *vri* meaning to count, classify, consider, describe or choose. For example, each letter of the alphabet is a *varna* (classification). Then, the roots *r* and *rn* mean enjoyment or pleasure. So *varna* indicates 'choosing with pleasure'. In other words, it signifies a classification based on free choice.

Dr S Radhakrishnan translates the IV, 13 part of the *Gita* as, "The fourfold order was created by Me according to the *gunas* – divisions of quality and work." He goes on to explain, "The emphasis is on *guna* (aptitude) and *karma* (function) and not *jati* (birth). The *varna* or order to which we belong to is independent of sex, birth or breeding."

The spirit of the early *varna* system deteriorated into a caste or *jati* system based on birth as Aryan domination over ancient India became stronger and the people in power wanted to maintain the 'superiority' of their breed. However, strongly though the Aryans wanted not to mix with the other races, there came about a lot of intermarriages. So the society elders devised a method to group these mixed offspring separately to uphold the purity of bloodlines and to smoothly administer their domain. They chose to put in place an intricate system of classification. The classes functioned much like medieval European guilds ensuring division of labour, providing for the training of apprentices and allowing manufacturers to achieve specialisations.

The *Mahabharata* gives us glimpses into that complex arrangement of hereditary grouping:

The son of a *Shudra* man upon a *Brahmin* woman became a *Chandala*. The son of a *Shudra* man upon a *Kshatriya* woman became a *Vratya*. The son of a *Shudra* man upon a *Vaishya* woman became a *Vaidya*. The son of a *Vaishya* man upon a *Brahmin* woman became a *Magadha*. The son of a *Vaishya* man upon a *Kshatriya* woman became a *Vamaka*. The son of a *Kshatriya* man upon a *Brahmin* woman became a *Suta*. Then, intermixing within the new groups created more castes.

Fortunately, the caste system, even in the *Mahabharata*'s time, was not very rigid. During his conversation with Naga Nahusha Yudhisthira says, "In human society, O mighty and highly intelligent Naga, it is difficult to ascertain one's caste because of promiscuous mixing among the four orders. This is my opinion. And the *rishis* must be having a similar view because they begin a sacrifice with such expressions as, 'Of whatever caste we may be, we celebrate the sacrifice.' Therefore those that are wise have asserted that **character is the chief and essential requisite in a man.**"

♦

Translator's Note C

The Status of Women in Sri Krishna's Time

During the *Mahabharata*'s time, the ideal of a woman's loyalty to her husband differed much from that of later times. It was customary, then, to acquire a son begotten by another man from one's wife, if one happened not to have a male heir. This was called *Niyoga* and was considered a method superior to adoption, which later on, replaced *Niyoga*. With the popularity of adoption, disappeared the tolerant attitude towards any lapse a woman might commit. Women who were rescued from the hands of the enemy and, perhaps, were used by them, were never abandoned. They were brought back into the family-fold and given their former status. This attitude was not due to compassion. A woman was a man's possession. Inability to protect her from the enemy and losing her was a matter of humiliation to him. In the *Ramayana*, Sita is abandoned by Rama for being a prisoner of Ravana. This happens only because the events of the *Ramayana* happened much later than the events of the *Mahabharata*. (Source: *Yuganta* by Irawati Karve.)

It is interesting to note the story Pandu related to Kunti to enlighten her on the subject of a woman's status in society:

"Dear Kunti," Pandu said, "In ancient times, all women were unbound and independent even after their marriage. They were allowed to mix with other men without any hesitation. We must accept that this is the law of life. All living beings, except the human species, are unrestricted in this matter. Oh fair-eyed one, not too long ago, there lived a *rishi* called Uddyaloka, whose son was Shvetaketu. Once upon a time, a Brahmin fondly holding Shvetaketu's mother's hand invited her to follow him on his journey. The mother went away with him.

Shvetaketu was furious. How could his mother go away with another man! His father, *Rishi* Uddyaloka, tried to soothe his son by saying that that was the law of nature. His father's explanations, however, fell on deaf ears. On that very day Shvetaketu made loyalty between husband and wife a strict edict of society."

The above story gives an interesting angle to human civilisation's long history of women's subjugation. Are the offspring to be blamed more for the situation than the husbands themselves?

✦

Translator's Note D

How Bhakti was Perceived in Mahabharata's Time

Hero-worship is the root of *Bhakti* — the sentiment of devotion. The devotee feels that the god-hero would rescue him from all difficulties. In the *Mahabharata*'s time, however, doing one's duty was more important than praying to one's gods. Perhaps, even temples were not in existence. The word *Devayatana* (god's house) is mentioned four times in the *Mahabharata*, but it seems they were all later additions. Also hymns in praise of Shiva, Vishnu and Sun God, which occur in the *Mahabharata* seem to be later interpolations. On the other hand, offerings to dead ancestors were made every month. The doctrine of *Karma* and the idea of rebirth were getting firmly established.

Life for the people was not nihilistic. It was not *Maya* or illusion as Shankaracharya had later (in 800 A.D.) propounded. It was harsh and hard but had to be faced bravely. There was no escape. According to Irawati Karve, the *Mahabharata* marks the end of an era for these reasons. "The pervading despair and frustration, hardness and realism of the *Mahabharata* never again appeared in Indian literature," Karve says.

However, *Bhakti*, even though not keenly adhered to by the general public during the time of the *Mahabharata* war, is a basic human emotion. From the point of human psychology, it is a component of love. The seed of *Bhakti* can be detected even in the earliest hymns of the world which were but inspired praises of natural elements.

From the *Mahabharata*, we find that Sri Krishna had a large fan-following, where the fans were almost like devotees to him. In that sense, we can say that *Bhaktimarga* had a tiny beginning during Krishna's time itself. In later years, it developed into a major source of artistic energy in India.

✦

Translator's Note E

Some Critical Comments on Bankim Chandra's Krishna Charitra

In his work, Bankim Chandra has shown how wonderfully self-controlled Sri Krishna was and how much he wanted 'the greatest good for the greatest number'. Yet he did not take into account some clear, historical pointers, which show that Krishna held the interest of the Yadavas closest to his heart and took care to do, first and foremost, everything that would benefit the Yadavas. For example, even though the Pandavas would have had other children, Parikshita, who had Yadava blood in him, was coroneted to the throne after the Pandavas. Then again, the Yadavas managed to avoid major loss of lives in the *Mahabharata* war by generally remaining non-combatants or abstaining from the war altogether.

Krishna had personal ambitions too. "Though he says in the *Gita* that he had no ambition or objective at all, yet he had, in reality... personal goals to attend," points out Irawati Karve. One of Krishna's special ambitions was to become a 'Vasudeva', a position approaching divinity, a title which could be borne only by one man in his age. In fact, he had a rival for the title – the mighty king of Pundra – who claimed to have all the signs of a Vasudeva (knowledge, lordship, potency, strength, virility and splendour). Pundra also professed to be the Sun God personified. Krishna, however, managed to kill him in a battle. That Krishna had a fancy for decorations can be supported by the fact that he did not decline to accept the honour given to him by Yudhisthira at his *Rajasuya Yajna*. Krishna himself could have nominated Bhishma for the credit. That he held Bhishma in very high esteem is proved by the fact that he made Bhishma, even when he was utterly wounded and dying, the Father of Yudhisthira's Constitution.

On the other side of the spectrum are critics of Krishna who hold that Krishna himself was personally responsible for the *Mahabharata* war. This assessment, of course, as Bankim Chandra has pointed out, is absolutely baseless. Anyone who has gone through the *Mahabharata* would admit that Sri Krishna had tried his best to stop the war from taking place. However, once war became inevitable, he wanted the party he had joined, to win.

On the whole, though, Bankim's study of Sri Krishna's character, even with its limitations, can be praised as a fascinating work of pioneering research.

◆

Appendix A

Rabindranath Tagore's Criticism of Bankim Chandra's Krishna Charitra

As we, the Indians, received English education for the first time ever, we began criticising our political system and seriously examining our social and religious set-ups. In every English educated student's mind arose discontent and doubt about his/her society and faith.

Reflections on the current situations of society and faith encouraged active involvement in those areas. However, though it is easy to express our opinion on any matter, it is not easy to act towards one's convictions. At present, we can do very little about the political state of our country as we are not the rulers. Therefore, it is quite acceptable if we do not stop our incisive and energetic criticisms of the political conditions of our time, though we cannot do anything about them. However, bringing about social and religious changes is quite in our own hands. So, when we feel that certain alterations are required in our religious and social systems, but do not do anything to bring them about, we have only ourselves to blame. Nevertheless, a human being would not like to remain guilt-ridden for a long time, nor is the emotion of guilt healthy for him. So, when we cannot do anything about them, we begin to validate even the defects of our society, ending up by announcing that our social norms were the most magnificent and wholesome in the world.

I do not claim that such behaviour is insincere or unnatural. In fact, religious and social norms have such deep roots in a nation's collective consciousness that any attempt to change them has to encounter resistance from many different quarters giving rise to new problems replacing the older ones. In such a situation, one tends to go back to passivity, maybe even more haughtily stating that that was a sign of one's efficiency instead of one's inefficiency.

At the time of such recessive journey of Bengali society's intellectual process was written Bankim Chandra's *Krishna Charitra*. When both minor and major voices of Bengal were together making a loud noise with saying nothing really significant a new utterance, a new melody of great talent made its presence felt. Bankim Chandra's *Krishna Charitra* was definitely not a mediocre creation. The work did not seek mass approval. Instead, it appealed to the masses to follow a disciplined path of a new approach.

If we analyse the way society was when *Krishna Charitra* was written and if we analyse the attitudes of Bankim's contemporaries, we cannot fail to notice how prominently his book stands out as a unique manifestation of a very powerful and original aptitude.

Bankim's strength of conviction that is manifested in the book is our permanent gain. Bengalis are in acute need of such strength. Even though at places, the book lacks good taste and fails to justify its propositions, it is a pillar of strength for our weak and timid community.

When even the learned citizens of our country were deluded and were blindly upholding whatever was written in the *shastras*, Bankim Chandra, in his *Krishna Charitra* bravely and proudly signalled the victory of independent and unbiased thinking. He examined the *shastras* in the light of history. He put even our well-known traditions under the scrutiny of investigation and revived rational thinking from its degraded position in society by giving it a regal status.

In our opinion, the primary subject of the book, *Krishna Charitra*, is not Krishna but independent thought and eagerness of mind. Firstly, in the book, Bankim counsels us not to passively follow the *shastras* or the social rituals when praying to God. We should instead, according to Bankim, consciously connect our religious practices with the noblest aspirations of our spirits. Secondly, in the book, Bankim maintains that only the believable parts of the scriptures can be called sacred. The unbelievable parts of the scriptures, according to him, should be ignored. Such distinctive ideas endow *Krishna Charitra* with a glorious spiritual force.

In the book, the author's aim is to prove the greatness of Krishna's character by supporting it by facts from history. He begins his work by his reflections on history.

This is the first instance where the character of Krishna has been studied from the perspective of history. The author had no precedence for his research as no one had ever taken up such an approach before him. Therefore, he had to take up the sole responsibility of selecting what should be considered as history and rejecting what should not. Clearly, before deciding what material can be classified as history a scholar has to take great pains in minutely examining and rejecting material that cannot be classified as history. In our opinion, in *Krishna Charitra*, Bankim has executed the function of rejection very successfully. However, his function of selecting facts, tagging them as historical events and convincingly reconstructing Krishna's character with them lacks thoroughness.

Bankim relies mainly on the *Mahabharata* for his work even after frankly admitting that it contained many interpolations. Unfortunately, he has failed to conclusively establish exactly which parts of that epic are genuine.

Bankim has discovered three distinct layers of the *Mahabharata*. According to him, the first layer has nobleness and poetic excellence in it; the second layer is less noble and contains some inferior poetry; the third layer consists entirely of random compositions inserted by various poets at various periods of time.

But my readers would understand that ranking the parts of a composition on the basis of their poetic merit can at best be only an approximation. Moreover, appreciation of poetry is a subjective matter. People can differ in their opinion of the same poem. Again, the same poet may not always maintain the same standard of fineness throughout any one of his compositions. We have examples where a single composition has its high and low points.

Thus, not the difference in poetic ability but only the difference in the use of language can provide a researcher clues to the dates of his subject matter. And, it is extremely difficult to examine the *Mahabharata* for such linguistic differences....

Secondly, a poet can write good poetry but that does not mean that he has to be historically sound. Ancient India was replete with innumerable hearsays about Kaurava and Pandava's rivalry. A talented poet, selecting some of the stories from that vast pool probably used them to compose his own creative work. Later, lesser poets could have inserted in that work what they knew to be genuine historical data. In such a situation, the lesser poets could be giving a more truthful account of the events. It is common knowledge that a good creative work often distorts history. If someone obsessed with truth were to put in correct historical facts in any of Shakespeare's plays, for example, its artistic coordination and beauty of characterisation could be severely damaged. So, I suppose, it is clear why no one would seriously expect that Shakespeare's original writings would provide historical data.

In any case, it is accepted that the *Mahabharata* contains the writings of many poets of various ages. But how to identify them, how to determine the time of their writings and how to assess their comparative historical validity are problems which have no solutions yet.

Still, nobody can disagree with Bankim Babu on what he says about unnatural elements in a composition. First of all, he says, supernatural incidents are not believable. Secondly, wherever any supernatural act has been described in a composition, there, almost certainly would be found a time gap between the original act and the description of it. Another sign that an incident was not based on history, Bankim points out, is to find it describing a great personality being worshipped as a god. Any such tract must have been added to the epic after the concerned personality's lifetime.

So, no historian should object to Bankim rejecting from Krishna's character elements which seem superhuman or supernatural. On the other hand, we do not totally approve of his rejecting some parts of the epic when they do not agree with other parts of it. For, a great man or a great event can give rise to diverse folklores. Poets can choose from those stories and modify them according to their own creative purpose. Thus, one poet may perceive Krishna as a dutiful and godly human being, while another may perceive him as a scheming politician. Though both the pictures may remain incomplete in their representation of Krishna, both may partially carry some truth in them. Indeed, it would be difficult to say which of the two accounts was more dependable.

So we do not think that the character of Krishna that Bankim has discovered by analysing and scrutinising Krishna's references in the

Mahabharata has a sufficiently dependable historical database. Bankim has himself said on several occasions that what Krishna says in the *Mahabharata* might not be the exact words of the real Krishna who once lived. The words, Bankim admits, were in fact, chosen by the poets who composed the epic to express their personal impressions of Krishna. Naturally, therefore, we cannot be sure that a poet was relating historical facts truthfully unless there were genuine proofs to support his text. We give you an example to elaborate what we mean. Bankim Babu says, "Kunti, remembering the sorrow of her sons and daughter-in-law wept a lot in Krishna's presence. Krishna consoled her in a very worthy way. Only somebody who knows human nature minutely and thoroughly can speak in that manner. Krishna said, 'The Pandava brothers, by conquering sleep, lethargy, hunger, thirst, cold, heat and merriment are relishing the joy of being brave. Sacrificing the pleasures of the senses they are immersed in the ecstasy of daring. Those mighty dauntless ones, full of enthusiasm, are never easily satisfied. Gallant men like them experience either acute pain or intense happiness. On the other hand, mediocre men, involved in the pleasures of the senses, who do not endeavour for the highest goals, remain unhappy. Conquering one's kingdom or living in the forests (achieving one's goal or doing whatever is necessary to achieve it) are both – bliss.'"

What Bankim has quoted from the *Mahabharata* is replete with deep human realisation. However, we do not believe that it reveals anything about Krishna, the person, who once really lived. Instead, it reflects the views of a particular poet of the *Mahabharata* who wrote it. It reveals his large-heartedness and his understanding of human nature. The quotation occurs in the ninth chapter of *Udyoga Parva*. Almost forty chapters later, Kunti relates an ancient story called Vidula and Sanjaya's story. In Kunti's story, spirited Vidula endeavours to enthuse her battle-weary son by impressing upon him the glory of his *Dharma – Kshatriya Dharma*. What she says is quite similar to Krishna's words quoted earlier. Vidula says, "Continue to think like a man. Do not disgrace your spirit, which has limitless energy, by trying to satiate it with insignificant things…. Tiny pots get easily filled with water. A tiny mouse can hold only a little amount of something in its fists. Similarly, a man who is not manly enough is satisfied with little…. It is a hundred times better to ignite for a moment than to keep emitting smoke forever without lighting up…. In the world around us, bright men hate things of meagre value. Poor quality goods, moreover, cause harm to even the person who prefers them.... The result of any human being's efforts is always uncertain. However, somebody who strives hard to reach his goal has a fair chance of succeeding, while somebody who never tries for his goal because he is scared of the uncertainty of the outcome will certainly never succeed."

From the above example, we find that a poet of the *Mahabharata* thought highly of dutifulness as a desirable human quality and had stressed his preference by many relevant examples. After studying the *Mahabharata* with enough care, we might even venture to think that the presenting of Kuru-Pandava's war in an epic form was mainly done to broadcast the importance of following one's duty actively (*karma-yoga*). The main characters of the *Mahabharata* – Krishna, Arjuna, Bhishma, Karna – are model *karmaveeras* (those who act diligently to fulfil their duties). Even Gandhari and Draupadi shine out in the glory of their dutifulness. To do the right thing, Gandhari had asked her husband to leave Duryodhana. Draupadi's understanding of duty had made her say "It is a sin to kill a person who should not be killed. Similarly, it is a sin not to kill a person who deserved to be killed."

But, again, from what Bankim has to say about Krishna, we only come to the conclusion that at one time some unknown poet's mental image of ideal greatness was very high and that he created the character of Krishna in the *Mahabharata* to match that high ideal. Possibly, Krishna is a person from history but we cannot prove that *Mahabharata*'s Krishna was entirely created in the likeness of that real Krishna. We find that even within the *Mahabharata*, different authors have tried to paint the character of Krishna according to their individual preferences.

In the matter of court cases, we can cross-check one witness's delivery by that of another witness's. However, in the case of the episodes of Krishna's life collected from the *Mahabharata*, we have no scope for cross-checking. For, as Bankim Babu has found out, the span of Krishna's life that is described in the *Mahabharata* is not described in any other scriptures, thus keeping no way open for anybody to verify what is claimed there about Krishna.

Bankim has examined the historicity of the *Mahabharata* mainly in the context of Krishna's life. However, his work would have been more satisfactory to us if he had selected the historically valid portions of the entire *Mahabharata* first, and had, then, confined his study of Krishna only to those portions....

For example, Bankim has expressed his doubts that Draupadi really had five husbands.... He says, "I, too, do not believe that Dhrupad had a daughter from the fire of a *Yajna*. However, it is possible that he had a biological daughter. And it is quite believable that this daughter had a *swayamvara sabha* for her marriage where Arjuna had shot the winning mark in archery. After that whether she had one husband or five is not important to us."

Actually, it is very important. Bankim accepts the *Mahabharata* as history and only on that basis, he believes that Krishna, as characterised in the *Mahabharata*, has historical credibility. Draupadi having five husbands comes up again and again in the narrative. But, if such a major happening was not historically true, then surely, it would weaken the claim to history of all the other portions of the *Mahabharata* where Draupadi is depicted as having five husbands. And, in those portions, whatever is said about Krishna will also become suspect. Automatically, it would reduce the overall chance of *Mahabharata*'s Krishna's historicity. When one has chosen to depend on a single account to draw one's conclusions, then before accepting some parts of that account as true, one needs to be sure that no part of that account is false.

However, if Bankim had been that careful in dealing with his subject, his Bengali readers would have been deprived of the good fortune of having *Krishna Charitra*. Even a whole lifetime would not be enough to properly root out all the unauthentic parts of the *Mahabharata*. That Bankim has started a narrow pathway into the jungle that is our *Mahabharata* is a wonder and a blessing for us. However, we have to admit that his work has remained incomplete. Now, we have to start where Bankim's talent has left us. He has not given us the perfect pearl but has shown us how we must jump into the ocean if we wanted to have it. Probably we would respond by saying, "Please, let us not jump into that ocean! We would rather be without the pearl."

Citing examples of the writings of Macaulay, Carlyle, LaMartine, Thucydides and others, Bankim calls the *Mahabharata* 'history written as a poem'. However, we call it 'a creative poem which borrows its material from history'. In any case, we are not anxious to find out whether our notion of Krishna's greatness comes from history or poetry or a combination of both. And, as we know, even history cannot be totally authentic. We have seen how difficult it is even for an eye-witness to grasp the true essence of events and to tender an exact portrayal of them. It is more difficult to draw a comprehensive picture of a personality or a sequence of events out of pieces of information.

We know that people can misjudge their own relatives or completely misunderstand their friends. It is more difficult to know a great person intimately. And, when one has to judge him from a distance or after a long period of time, much inaccuracy can come into that judgement. Various artists can craft figures differing from one another of the same great person, selecting facts and legends according to each one's separate penchants. And, people from the general public are also free to determine, according to their own private tastes, which figure should be considered closest to the original model. Thus our perception of history depends largely on the historians' conjectures and our own beliefs.

Amid such a state of confusion it is quite possible for a poet to get nearer to the truth of an issue than a historian.... At one time in ancient India, various legends and hearsays about the Kurukshetra war had become popular. Then, a poet, collecting all those bits and pieces compiled a beautiful whole using his own power of imagination. We cannot claim that his would be a lesser truth than a historian's.

Facts, in themselves, are insignificant when compared to truth. We have to find truth from facts with the help of logic and imagination. Many a time, a book of history can be only a collection of facts while a poet, with his imagination, can reveal the truth beautifully. Therefore, we think it is useless and impossible to look into a poetic work like the *Mahabharata* to find out what really had happened many many years ago. Mr Frude, a scholar of ancient studies has said, "Prose cannot describe the greatness of a genuinely mighty person. It can be done only by poetry. Whatever might be the reason for it, this is really the case. Poetry has the power to revive. Prose doesn't have it. This is the reason why poets are the true historians."

We take the words of Frude to mean that a list of a great man's activities will only be a datasheet unless a sensitive mind can realise the essence of his greatness and reveal that truth for the common man....

The majesty of Krishna that is revealed by the original poet of the *Mahabharata* is the most valuable truth about him. That truth gets imprinted in the minds of the readers of the *Mahabharata* and cannot be tarnished by the fact that what Krishna says and does in the epic cannot all be proven....

There is no doubt that many ordinary facts of Krishna's life were rejected in building the character of the *Mahabharata*'s Krishna and only those facts which corresponded with his true nature were selected. And, conversely, words that Krishna, the real person, had not spoken, acts that Krishna, the real person, had not performed, have been assigned to *Mahabharata*'s Krishna to highlight his characteristics. This has made *Mahabharata*'s Krishna more convincing than the person he really was. So, the original poet of the *Mahabharata* has captured the true spirit of Krishna for us by building on his own impression of Krishna's greatness. By doing that, he has made his Krishna more authentic than the historical Krishna.

Now that Bankim wants to establish Krishna's nobility among his readers, his task should have been just to quote for them how the original poet of the *Mahabharata* had pictured him.... Unfortunately, instead of objectively doing that, Bankim, presupposing that the *Mahabharata*'s poet's idea of Krishna should match with his own idea of Krishna, sets about looking for such similarities. We cannot evaluate Bankim's success with his method unless we scan the entire *Mahabharata* ourselves. However, for the time being, I want to draw my readers' attention to just one anomaly.

Whom Bankim calls the poet of the first layer of the *Mahabharata* did not believe in Krishna's divinity and Bankim has admitted that. He even believed that this fact was one of the best markers to identify the first layer of the *Mahabharata*.

Yet, Bankim himself believed in Krishna's divinity. This difference made the work of tracing down the original poet's idea of Krishna from the *Mahabharata* difficult for Bankim. Bankim was constantly influenced by his own idea of Krishna and was looking for signs in the *Mahabharata*'s Krishna to conform with his own idea of the hero.... In his book, *Dharmatatva*, Bankim has established his theory of *Dharma*. Now, with *Krishna Charitra*, he wished to give that theory a practical and human dimension. With his mind occupied with such a desire, anybody would find it difficult to impartially discover another poet's vision.

Some of you may remind me that even though Bankim believed in Krishna's divinity, he has said over and over again that as a human *avatar*, Krishna would act only within the limits of human capability, that he would not display his supernatural power to prove his godliness. So Bankim, after all, wanted to discover Krishna the man and not Krishna the god.

However, the human being he wanted to discover in Krishna would have to be without any imperfections and his emotions would have to be perfectly balanced. In other words, he would have to be the image of a theory. But probably the Krishna of the *Mahabharata*'s poet was not that.

The original poet of the *Mahabharata* did not create a human character to personify a theory or some rules of ethics. He had too much poetic merit to do that. He has, unlike lesser poets, dared to make even his super-heroes do petty things….

If the poet of the first layer of the *Mahabharata* did not believe Krishna to be a god, then we suppose, he would not have any reason to create him as an example of a highly moral person. Bankim has decided that the original poet of the *Mahabharata* was a great poet. Further, by deciding that a great poet like him would not put negative attributes in Krishna's character, has rejected all such portions of the epic as unoriginal. We claim that negativity and lack of balance are not signs to judge a character's superiority in a creative work. The character of Hamlet is quite faulty…. But nobody would doubt that it is a supremely spontaneous literary creation.

By removing every negative aspect from the character of *Mahabharata*'s Krishna, Bankim claims to have discovered the Krishna that the original poet of the epic had conceived. We have serious doubts about this claim.

But now I have to say something. It hardly matters that Bankim's idea of Krishna does not match with the *Mahabharata*'s poet's idea of him. The Bengali readership should consider itself blessed because Bankim had a noble idea.

As Frude has said, history cannot reveal a great person's majesty but poetry can. The idea of that majesty should be made to touch the reader's sensibilities as a vivid and wholesome experience. Debate and arguments can convey only a part of that idea to the readers. And, even that part would be in bits and pieces.

From the very beginning, Bankim approaches his subject sword in hand! So, he misses the chance of calmly upholding the image of Krishna before us.

We cannot blame Bankim for that, however, for people not devoted to Krishna and even some who are devoted to him mistakenly hold many wrong notions of the deity. Bankim had to clear such a cluttered ground first... to make room for setting up his idol of Krishna. The author successfully demonstrates to us in his *Krishna Charitra* how vastly different the real and pragmatic Krishna was from the general impression we have of him.

Unfortunately, Bankim also engages in many unnecessary confrontations while writing his book. We are deeply saddened by these quarrels. Bankim has written this book with a noble purpose in mind. To honour that purpose, he should have used ideas and words inspired by nobleness. Petty arguments and small-minded criticisms were bound to disturb the steady and calm state of mind that his work demanded. Many of the arguments are only made for magazines and periodicals. They are not suitable for a memorable work of paramount importance.

The author has used words like, 'foreign idiots', and has belittled Western scholars in many passages. Firstly, what he has done is wrong in its basic principle. Secondly, it is absolutely unsuitable for a valuable book. Unnecessarily ill-treating someone in the presence of a great dignitary amounts to lowering that dignitary's position.... Bankim has done just that by getting agitated over his differences of opinion with the Europeans. Wanting to establish Krishna's glory, he has ended up dishonouring him by losing his patience with the Europeans while writing about him. Bankim has expressed ill-feeling not only towards the European scholars but also towards the European race in general. I give you one or two examples:

"On hearing Shishupala's expletives for him, the merciful Krishna... remained silent even though he had enough power to kill the culprit that very moment.... He ignored Shishupala's verbal attacks completely. He did not feel the need to loudly announce like the Europeans, 'Forgiveness is a major *Dharma*. So I forgive you.'"

Taunting the Europeans to uphold Krishna's mercifulness has no justification. On top of that, it weakens the very purpose of Bankim's writing the passage. For, instead of putting the readers' mind into a calm frame so that they could fully apprehend the splendour of Krishna's mercifulness, it does just the opposite. A work like *Krishna Charitra* should not be written only for the modern Hindus but should be expected to be read through generations of people irrespective of their races.

My readers can easily understand what an unfavourable reaction a European reader would have while going through the passage I object to. I wonder who gave Bankim the impression that before forgiving someone, a European person always lectures on the merits of forgiveness. On the contrary, our own scriptures contain many instances of strange lectures. Nabbing Vasistha's cow, Vishvamitra was taking her away when she frantically called Vasistha to save her. But Vasistha said... "A merciful *Brahmin*, what can I do to save you when king Vishvamitra himself is taking you away? ....A *Kshatriya*'s strength is aggressiveness but a *Brahmin*'s strength is forgiveness. I am, therefore, very keen to observe forgiveness."

"People who love sensual pleasures can get them easily but they rarely become happy. Real happiness consists of winning a kingdom or living in the forest trying desperately to win that kingdom." Quoting Sri Krishna's words in the given passage, Bankim says, "We have such great sayings in Hindu *Puranas* and *Itihasas* and yet ignoring them prefer to read novels written by European women...."

Such impatient outbursts from Bankim, over and over again, in a major work like *Krishna Charitra*, are totally uncalled for. On the whole, in Bankim's work language, style and the development of thought do not complement one another to sustain a dignified, noble and gracious tone. This lack of co-ordination threatens to diminish even the brilliance of his magnificent subject matter – the character of Krishna.

At the slightest provocation, Bankim has quarrelled with the Europeans as well as the general readers. People who had the misfortune of having an outlook different from him in any matter have become his instant targets. Not only is his quarrelsome attitude unsuitable for the sublime theme he deals with, but also for the proper understanding of his work by the readers. The quarrels never fail to confuse them!

Bankim primarily wants to establish Krishna as the best of human beings. Yet he also raises the controversial, and in this case unnecessary, question of whether it was possible for God to be born on earth as an *avatar*. Worst, Bankim has not even given that argument any proper and conclusive ending.

Bankim answers his readers who ask him how can God, an abstract concept, take a human shape simply by saying that that is possible since God is all-powerful. "But is it necessary for God to take a human shape?" may ask other readers, "If he is all-powerful then he can, surely, destroy rogues like Ravana, Kumbhakarna, Kansa or Shishupala just by wishing them to die." Bankim's answer to such a question is that God incarnates not just to kill wicked people but also to set an example by His activities for human beings to follow.... This may raise the third question, "If God is all-powerful and if setting an example for human beings to follow is one of His aims, can't He create an ideal man to fulfil that role instead of Himself coming down to earth?" Bankim has neither raised the third question nor given a satisfactory answer to it.

The above arguments, however, does little to promote the purpose of Bankim's book. Bankim has admitted from time to time in the course of his work that a human ideal is a better guide for human beings to follow than a divine ideal. For, we might easily decide that it was futile to imitate an all-powerful being but what another human being does we hope and believe we can also do. By insisting on Krishna to be divine, Bankim has diminished the value of Krishna's humanity. When, with godly power, Krishna would be able to do anything, his feats would not particularly fascinate or inspire us.

Bankim has examined many social issues in his book which has done nothing to his thesis except to unnecessarily complicate it. In the chapter called, 'Polygamy of Krishna', Bankim has proposed that Krishna had taken only one wife, Rukmini. Unfortunately, after that, the author goes on to insist that polygamy was not always undesirable....

When, according to Bankim, Krishna had not married more than once, where was the need to build up a debate on polygamy? And, alas! Bankim has, again, failed to provide a proper conclusion to the debate.

Soon after this, to prove that the capture of Subhadra by Arjuna was not a blame-worthy move, Bankim refers to a Parsi gentleman named

Malabari. In all probability that poor Parsi's fame would fade away with paper-eating insects consuming the few old newspapers carrying his name. Yet, taunting him, Bankim has begun another of his social debates. And this time, too, has failed to conclude the dispute satisfactorily....

If Bankim had not insisted that Krishna was divine and if he had not clung to his pet theory of Krishna having the finest possible balance of emotional make-up, he would not have to get into arguments and frictions. He would have, then, done his work with an un-agitated mind. With a calm and objective outlook, Bankim could have unveiled the Krishna of the original poet of the *Mahabharata*. Bankim could have, then, placed his findings before his readers with confidence. In that case, in the course of his writing, he would not have to aggressively grapple with the scepticisms he foresaw his book to encounter. Then he could have maintained in his work the even tone of high literature.

What an actor is depicting on stage cannot be properly followed when a commentator is voicing his own personal interpretations from backstage. Similarly, Krishna's character in Bankim's *Krishna Charitra* has lost its vividness because of the author's constant arguments and debates. Bankim might insist that his *Krishna Charitra* was not meant for a stage performance – that it was, rather, a behind-the-scene job. His primary intention was to accumulate, Bankim might claim, the various elements Krishna would have in him to be an ideal human being. In other words, Bankim's endeavours were like that of a stage manager who had taken great pains to bring together the various pieces of the costume Krishna would need to dress up for the stage in his role of an ideal human being. Any other poet was now free to use that model to entertain the audience. By accepting Bankim's replica for his own use instead of trying to build another model, that poet could save a lot of contemplation, deliberation and physical enterprise.

The above article was published in Adhunik Sahitya, bearing the name Krishna Charitra, in 1895 – two years after Bankim Chandra's death.

✦

Appendix B

Bankim Chandra's Defence against Tagore's Criticism

Bankim's Krishna Charitra was criticised by Tagore for the first time in 1884, long before his comprehensive critical essay on the subject was published (in 1895). At the time of that first criticism, Bankim Chandra was 46 years old and Tagore was only 23 – half his age! In his reply to that earlier criticism, while defending his work, Bankim has demonstrated great patience, elder brotherly affection and forgiveness for the young poet and immense appreciation for his talents. The following is the translation of what he wrote in Bengali:

Recently there was a talk by Rabindranath Tagore… which was also published in *Bharati* magazine. The article has directly targeted me. This is nothing unusual. Such misfortunes have come my way even before Babu Rabindranath had learnt his alphabet. So far I have not reacted to them. However, on this occasion, I thought it was necessary to react. If I do not do that, people who trust me would be harmed.

…Babu Rabindranath is talented and highly educated. He writes beautifully and is good-natured as a person. I admire him, love him and care for him. If he has a few words of criticism for me, I consider it my duty to keep silent. I write these few pages only because I detect a shadow behind the sun that is Rabindranath….

According to Babu Rabindranath, I advise my readers to abandon truth for falsity wherever necessary. Indeed, he accuses me for worse crime than that. He says, "A foremost writer of our country openly, without any hesitation or fear, equates truth and falsehood and has expressed doubt about the real value of truth. Unfortunately, readers from the entire nation have silently, without opposing, listened to him.... The roots of our social values (*Dharma*) must have degenerated very badly for someone to dare to hit his axe right at its source, etc etc."

No doubt that the above statements speak of grave dangers. It appears that without Adi Brahma Samaj's healing effects, my influence would have badly corrupted the society. My readers may curiously wonder when had I openly told the common pedestrian to embrace falsity in lieu of truth. Unfortunately, I am unable to find out for them any such portion from my writings. I had hoped that Babu Rabindranath would help us in this matter but he has omitted to do that. From his 20 printed columns of speech, I found only six lines referring vaguely to the issue. I quote what he has said there:

"The respected writer (i.e., myself) imagines the character of an ideal Hindu and says, 'When he lies, it is only like *Mahabharata*'s Krishna who had lied for the benefit of the general public. In other words, the ideal Hindu lies when he thinks his lie is the truth.'"

I assure my readers that irrespective of who speaks it – myself or Sri Krishna – a lie can never become truth. Perhaps only a few chosen members of the Adi Brahma Samaj can perform that feat considering that they have used the word 'imagine' in quoting me when I have not used it in my original writing. My article published in the first issue of *Prachar* and titled *Hindu Dharma*, which Babu Rabindranath analyses here, compares two real Hindu personalities. That is not equivalent to imagining. Secondly, in that article, I have nowhere used or inferred the word 'ideal' of which I am accused of....

But let us not concern ourselves with such petty differences. Let us quickly come to the main issue. Has my statement, "Where a lie is truth", has any meaning at all? Does it not sound as useless as, "A square circle"? Obviously Babu Rabindranath has sensed that I have used my statement not in its bogus, literal meaning but with a special, suggestive connotation. That is the reason why he has taken it seriously enough to structure a lecture on it. However, did he sincerely try to understand in what special sense was the phrase used? If he did not, then it can be said that his aim is just to humiliate me instead of honestly wanting to investigate the underlying truth of the matter.

...I have based my statement that sometimes a lie can be taken as truth on some words that Sri Krishna had spoken.... If Babu Rabindranath had asked me I could have shown him where, in the *Mahabharata*, Sri Krishna had uttered those particular words. Now, let me explain, in short, the essence of Krishna's message to my readers:

Defeated by Karna in the battlefield, Yudhisthira had retreated to camp and had taken to bed. Soon, worrying for him, Krishna and Arjuna visited him. Anxious about Karna's might, Yudhisthira was hoping that Arjuna had killed him already. On hearing that Karna was still alive, he lost his temper. He scolded Arjuna for not felling Karna still and belittled Arjuna's *Gandiva* bow. Earlier Arjuna had taken a vow to kill anybody who dishonoured *Gandiva*. So now, to uphold the 'truth' of his vow, he would have to kill Yudhisthira. Arjuna decided to kill his elder brother and then to commit suicide to punish himself for that. Fortunately, Krishna rubbished Arjuna's way of thinking. He convinced his disciple that in such a case, observing his vow did not amount to upholding the truth. Here, Krishna said, not observing his vow was Arjuna's *Dharma* and what apparently was 'falsehood' (i.e., not keeping one's word) was truth.

Babu Rabindranath has used the words 'truth' and 'falsehood' in their literal, English usages whereas I have used the words in their Indian context. To my mind, our tendency to translate all our thoughts into English is a hurdle to our originality, aspiration and progress. I have used the words truth and falsehood in the sense they are used in India since ancient times. In its indigenous meaning, truth expresses something more than the English word 'truth'. In that Indian sense, keeping one's vow or word is also truth.

The Old English word 'troth' was often used in a similar sense. Troth is the origin of the modern English word 'truth'. The new word, truth, however, has taken on a different meaning while what was meant by troth is now expressed by words like honour and faith. Even thieves and scoundrels can have these qualities. Sinners can have these qualities. Truth, in the sense in which Babu Rabindranath has used it, can never be associated with sin.

Now, may I ask Babu Rabindranath and his associates if they sincerely think that Arjuna should have killed his elder brother (which would be a sin) just to honour his own innocent vow? If, waking up one morning someone vows to perform every possible crime in a day – murder, loot, adultery, torturing people – would my esteemed critics advise him to go ahead with his project simply for the sake of upholding the truth? If not, then they have to admit that in this case also, not being true to one's word is *Dharma* – the opposite is *Adharma* or falsity.

I hope now no argument will arise about my use of the words truth and falsehood to express what I meant. I do not believe that an Indian word derived from Sanskrit should leave its original meaning behind to be able to exactly correspond to its translatable version of English.

....I have just a few more words for Babu Rabindranath. Like everyone else, I have great regard for truth. What I hate is any kind of pretence. I hate the shorn-headed *vairagi* who sings 'truth, truth' but has a dishonest heart....

Pardon me for criticising Babu Rabindranath. I do this because I have great faith for his talent. Even at such a young age, he has made the Bengalis proud. My blessings are with him. May he live a long and meritorious life contributing immensely to our country's progress.

◆

Appendix C

Bankim Chandra's Study of Sri Krishna in Literature

The literature of any country is always influenced by its social changes. In India, the social conditions described in the *Ramayana* are different from the social conditions described in the *Mahabharata*, which are again different from the social conditions referred to in Kalidasa's writings.

Krishna is the hero of **Vidyapati**, a comparatively modern writer of Bengal. But in the past, he was also the hero of poet **Jaidev**. Earlier he was the hero of the **Madbhagavata**. However, the first mention of Krishna is found in the **Mahabharata**. So, let us view how Krishna was depicted in each of the four periods represented by the highlighted works/poets.

Let me clarify at the outset that the characterisation of a literary hero is never just the result of the social situations of the poet's lifetime. It also depends on the individual temperament of the poet himself. And, of course, it depends on which country (or part of the country) the poet belongs to. In other words, we can say that the work of a poet is dominated by three factors — the poet's nationality/regional identity, the social environment of his time, and his personal characteristics. If the images of Krishna created during each of the four time periods under our discussion differ from one another, we have to accept that all the three factors influencing the image of a literary hero have played their roles in it. However, in this essay, I will speak only of the social differences that influenced Krishna's figure from time to time.

It is not yet clear when the original story of the *Mahabharata* was composed. That it came before the *Madbhagavata* cannot be denied. One can be sure of this by just comparing the language of the two. The Sanskrit used in the *Madbhagavata* is comparatively modern. So are its styles of rhythm and verses.

The *Mahabharata*, without doubt, carries the first description of Vasudeva Krishna.[9] When one reads the *Mahabharata* one feels that ancient India was, then, going through its third phase of social transition. The ages of *Satya* and *Treta* had past. In the *Satya Yuga*, the newly arrived Aryan tribes in India were busy making their homes in the basins of Saraswati and Drishadwati rivers. They, at that time, observed a simple, rustic religious practice, which they thought would protect them from barbarian vandals. Their religious code, then, consisted merely of invoking powerful natural entities like the sun and the wind and praying to them for their support and blessings.

In the *Treta Yuga*, the population of the Aryan settlers had increased. They had overcome and subdued the barbarians, in the process becoming powerful warriors themselves. They had built cities like Varanasi, Ayodhya and Mithila on their conquered land. In these cities, art, craftsmanship and various branches of knowledge flourished. The Aryans of India had also secured the boundaries of their domain. Now, it was time for them to enjoy the assets they had accumulated. But the question was, how would they divide the spoils of war among themselves? How would the prosperity won by all, be shared? As there was no clear answer to that question, internal strife was inevitable. This was also the moment of birth of the *Dvapara Yuga*. The epic *Mahabharata* is a product of that conflict-ridden *Dvapara*.

In a troubled social situation, two types of personalities acquired prominence – the brave warrior wanting to subdue his peers, and the political adviser capable of guiding the people who hold power. In the

---

[9] *Translator's Footnote*
Namesake seer Krishna, author of *Taittirya Brahmana* in *Krishna Yajur Veda*, flourished a few thousand years earlier, in the Vedic era.

Mahabharata, the first type is represented by Arjuna, and the second by Krishna.

The characterisation of Krishna found in the *Mahabharata* has no comparison in world literature. The love-play of Vraja, which is the substance of Jaidev's and Vidyapati's writings and is an important element of the *Madbhagavata*, is totally absent from the *Mahabharata*. In the *Mahabharata*, Krishna is a first-rate statesman. With godly sagacity, he successfully conceives the method of building an empire. His foresight is unparalleled. He wins the reputation of being a divine incarnation as nobody is capable of fathoming the depth of his wisdom. From the moment he appears on the scene, he becomes the prime decision-maker – a robust but a patient thinker.

During Krishna's time, India was divided into numerous small kingdoms. Their differences and clashes had made the country weak. Krishna realised that a major war would bring about a welcome change in the political composition of the country – that it would give rise to one, righteous empire. In the Kurukshetra war, Krishna supported the deserving party but did not take up arms himself. He did not want to project himself as overtly partial, for he was ever-tactful. Krishna's later image of a pleasure-seeking cowherd boy is nowhere to be found in the *Mahabharata*.

As the years went by, various philosophical thoughts developed in India. The sophisticated classes of the society questioned the validity of worshipping each and every natural phenomenon separately, for they felt that one single source of power was the cause of their energy. Some people said that the source of energy was God. Some said there was only energy and nothing called God. Some said God was separate from the physical world, while others said that the physical world was a part of God. Hinduism was riddled with confusion, as many branches of philosophy developed with their own favourite theories. In frustration, half of India turned to Buddhism.

Then, hundreds of years later, the author of the *Madbhagavata* tried to revive Hinduism through his poetry. He was a philosopher-poet and he based his work on the most popular branch of Hindu philosophy – the Sankhya philosophy. This system of thought describes the Universe as a kind of rendezvous of the male and the female aspects (*Purusha* and *Prakriti*) of creation.

The author of the *Madbhagavata* selected Krishna as his hero because he was already believed by many to be an incarnation of God. And he created the pretty, amorous *gopis* (milkmaids)[10], representing womanhood, from his own poetic imagination. His work allegorically depicts the journey of the soul. The soul (the male aspect of creation) meets nature (the female aspect of creation) but has to, inevitably, leave her again, in order to blend with the boundless, formless freedom (*Mukti*). Their meetings are out of wedlock, because everything earthly is imperfect and painful.

The richness of philosophical allegory is totally missing from Jaidev's compositions. Aryan civilisation, in Jaidev's time, was going through a phase of decadence. Ritualism had replaced noble thinking. The social elite had become pleasure-loving. They enjoyed domestic comfort and soothing entertainment. Glamour was attractive. Dance and music were sought-after skills.

The *Gitagovinda* is an outcome of that society. In it, the image of Krishna, the hero, is of a charming young man, a pleasure-loving, fun-loving boy. Radha (who first appeared in *Brahmavaivarta Purana*), in the *Gitagovinda* is a bewitching lady. The work is superb for its lyrics. But the honour and prestige bestowed upon Krishna's character in the *Mahabharata* and the *Madbhagavata* are missing completely from the *Gitagovinda*.

Later, Bengal was invaded by the Muslims. Islam became the dominant religion of the region. But soon Raghunatha and Chaitanya

---

[10] *Translator's Footnote*
In his text, Bankim uses the word 'Radha' and not *gopi* in this particular sentence, even though in his longer *Krishna Charitra*, he has particularly stated that Radha's name did not appear in *Madbhagavata*. Bankim's use of the name of Radha, in the present context, may have resulted from either of the following two reasons:
- By Radha he simply meant *gopis* in general.
- This was a mistake on Bankim's part. It is possible that Bankim's research on his subject-matter was not yet as comprehensive as it would be when he, later, wrote the longer version of *Krishna Charitra*.

Deva came forward as saviours of Hinduism. The poet Vidyapati was a predecessor of Chaitanya. He was the first flame of the revivalists. In his compositions, the basic imagery of Radha and Krishna is the same as in the *Gitagovinda*, but has new shades of colour. In the *Gitagovinda*, Krishna's character is superficial. Vidyapati gives it the depth of inner serenity. The mood of Jaidev's social environment was predominantly happy. The mood of Vidyapati's social environment was predominantly sad. That sadness is reflected in Vidyapati's work.